Dog Tags Yapping

Dog Tags Yapping

The World War II Letters of a Combat GI

M. D. Elevitch

With a Foreword by
Jean Van Doren

Southern Illinois University Press
Carbondale

06 05 04 03 4 3 2 1

The author will donate earnings from this publication
to veterans' organizations and projects.

Library of Congress Cataloging-in-Publication Data

Elevitch, M. D. (Morton D.)
Dog tags yapping : the World War II letters of a combat GI /
M. D. Elevitch, With a Foreword by Jean Van Doren.
    p. cm.
    1. Elevitch, M. D. (Morton D.) 2. World War,
1939–1945—Personal narratives, American. 3. Soldiers—
United States—Correspondence. I. Title.
D811.E553A3 2003
940.54'1273'092—dc21
ISBN 0-8093-2527-6 (cloth : alk. paper)   2002154371

Printed on recycled paper. ♻

The paper used in this publication meets the minimum re-
quirements of American National Standard for Information
Sciences—Permanence of Paper for Printed Library Materials,
ANSI Z39.48-1992. ♾

To the memory of

John Fanset and Thomas Walters,

killed in action in Germany,

January 1945

Contents

Foreword: The Prisoner's Box

In 1943 the families of America were cautiously hopeful that the war would end within two or three years. June's high school graduation classes still sent their boys as military inductees, though.

Morton Elevitch was just one; eighteen, red-haired, naive, and energetic, he wrote on sports for his Duluth, Minnesota, high school's newspaper and acted with its radio drama group. He had expected to be in the army's specialized college program, ASTP, but instead he found himself braving the army's chaos. He wrote his letters home to three persons only: Papa, in the "Big House"; Mom — parents were divorced; and younger brother "Burr," all of whom he addressed with dozens of zany names and salutations.

These letters were peppered with cartoons — no art lessons ever — passed by the censors, and eventually stayed stashed in an apartment house basement along with his Purple Heart and oak-leaf cluster, in a wooden box made for cigarettes exchange by a German prisoner of war in the stockade "guarded" by Pfc Elevitch.

Fifty-four years later, a friend of twenty-odd years' standing saw these letters and was stunned by the quality of writing and the hasty cartoons. I am that friend, and I've convinced ex-Pfc Elevitch to let the general public read these hilarious, informative, whimsical, historical, and outrageous letters that, together, make up this sensitive personal history.

The long dormant letters are a revealing chronicle of a boy's forced growth as an infantryman in the European theater. He was sixteen when Franklin Delano Roosevelt's "Day of Infamy" speech was piped into the stony-silenced auditorium of Duluth Central High School the day after the Japanese bombed Pearl Harbor on December 7, 1941. (War wasn't new to him; Edward R. Murrow's "This Is London" radio broadcasts on the Battle of Britain that autumn had already caused a slight shift in America's preference for isolation. Before that, listeners were unnerved, shockingly aware of the Nazis mowing down and annexing Europe.)

But the parents of these midwestern high school boys were wary at best. After Pearl Harbor, they braced themselves, as did all of America. Boys left Duluth for service. Gold stars on white satin hung in some windows: killed in action.

Two years after the Day of Infamy speech, Private Morton Elevitch arrived in southern Georgia at Fort Benning for training. His induction had been swift. A short commute to St. Paul was all he needed to swear his allegiance. Leaving Duluth a draftee, returning the next day a soldier was perplexing; and there would be more sudden, even calamitous, changes before his letters were gathered in the box.

Jean Van Doren

Prisoner's box. Photo by Philip James Herman.

Introduction: The Individualist

I am the 2nd man in the 3rd squad of the 1st platoon of the 7th company of the 2nd Battalion of the 5th Training Regiment of ASTP.
— "Garbled Information"

When these letters came out for an airing, I did not know they would stay out. They had been packed away as tightly and irrevocably as the soldier in the quote above. But Jean Van Doren, my motivator (one of many who deserve tributes), urged me to respond to a notice in a local Nyack, New York, paper. Florida State University wanted to preserve the memorabilia of those who "gallantly" served in World War II. I was more than willing to separate myself from the not-so-beloved items that had been in my prisoner's box for so many years (protected, that is, by the handiwork of a German, one of the "enemy"). In all that time, I had neither been interested in nor read accounts of war, not even my own war, and though in 1960 I founded and published a magazine devoted to the personal narrative—diaries, journals, letters—I had not thought to look at my own letters. But stimulated by the trumpets sounding off about me—from Stephen Ambrose, Tom Brokaw, Steven Spielberg—I began untying the bundles, many wound with broad shoelaces from GI shoes—and found they were in perfect condition.

Three batches subsequently went to Florida. Then for many months the letters were sorted and shuffled into a coherent binderful. It was not a labor of love. I could not remember, could not place, the actual events so graphically revealed in the letters, and still can't, at least not most of them. Luckily I have my 376th Regimental History to pinpoint what I was doing and where. Army papers such as *Yank* and *Stars and Stripes* were widely and continually circulated, yet nowhere do the letters touch on the general phases of the war. It was all a "dream." "Another dream has passed," I wrote after surviving one of many excruciatingly real events.

That was the method apparently: he—I—as witness. He sent his letters forth as good soldiers. Dream or not, they are on the mark, unrelenting, surprisingly debonair, his concern for his brother, his parents, his fellows manifest. He is always reassuring, no matter how rigorous the exercise—"I must be an individualist," he writes (in contrast to the regimentation at the head of this account). And he was company cartoonist—able to put everything in a bearable light for the home front and for those nearby who needed embellishment. (I do remember that.)

His nickname as a child was "Sunny"—no, I won't blush at that. A letter he wrote from Fort Benning, Georgia, shows his optimism. It is scribbled on the back of an orientation pamphlet for ASTP—one of the Army's most farsighted and ambitious programs. He and his thousands of college-bound comrades had joined their training units late: combat preparation had begun in Georgia and Mississippi many months before. Yet the delay did not turn simply into catch-up: these young men were to excel under horrendous conditions and to prove themselves as replacements for frontline troops drained away by the initial drives in Europe and the Battle of the Bulge. "The army is a wonderful thing," he writes on the pamphlet in the midst of a sober conversation with a new friend, Jack Fanset of Watertown, South Dakota, who tragically (and prophetically) is not to see the postwar world they discuss.

While I was not bitter, I did feel and retain emotions generated by the bouts with World War II and with myself (testing, testing what kind of person I should be). They were stored up and broke loose finally in a torrent of tears some twenty-four years after the war. We were in San Francisco. It was the week late in March 1969 when my first child, son Nikolas, was born, that in itself a cause for emotional unloading. Then at week's end General Eisenhower died, triggering those tears not for that worthy himself or his fatherly presence but, as I can make it out now, for my lost innocence, the lost years, the lost lives. Nothing like it since. Except the letters: they will say it for me. Back in service again.

Every day in uniform was momentous for "Privitch Elevate"—at least by my bleak but coveted Minnesota standards—and clamored for paper. Even in the jungle of an absurdly turgid night problem, he smiles, "thinking how I would write this to you." That writing fever takes him through the shooting war to the waiting war afterward in France, where he guards prisoners and longs for his own release. "It's much easier to wield a melancholy pen than to sit down and cry," he declares to his father.

With all its monolithic restraints, the Army nevertheless gave me the freedom and incentive to keep those home-obsessed letters in play, supplying and promoting endless opportunities—the rec halls, the passes, the movies, the special editions of books, the rest areas, and of course those high-flying, reliable V-mails that it conducted from us like so many formations of geese.

I ventured into set pieces, usually sent to my brother, in various writing styles and fictional forms: "Spray," "Proclamation," "Concerto for Two Spoons," the last one exuberant from the convalescent hospital when I knew my battle was done. I also could be a deliberate and precise recorder of death and that battle in "IT" and a summarizer of all that passed for me from training to ve day in "Soldier's Saga."

Intended only for a select and familiar few, my salutations are mainly warm-up words or rather nonwords—though not always. Many openings, to my mother, are particularly poignant: "Orchid Dew," "Violet Sparrow," "Dusk Hue." Almost never do I conclude with the conventional "love"—except in my "farewell letter," not a performance like so many others, when my last love is to be a monument and a gift.

I have not rewritten any letter. In some instances, I have rearranged parts of them or have omitted repetitions and other extraneous material to ensure narrative flow. Generally I have not corrected lapses in spelling. There is a wistful (Mortifying) irony in my asking brother Burr for "a good dictionery" (*sic,* and welcome to it). I stay by my side then, respectful of the boyish voice—direct, fresh, lively, and with a levity not overreaching to a youthful self nor misplaced when friends die (a barricade for shock?), consistently borrowed from influences such as Damon Runyon, the master of Guys and Dolls, the only one in the letters I can identify for sure, whose florid low-life lingo should have been as discordant to me as the war itself. But understandable if I thought I was bursting the mold as an individualist. Finding these letters and offering them, I am grateful I entered that wild bivouac of the mind.

Dog Tags Yapping

1

A Practice GI: Georgia and Mississippi, October 1943–July 1944

[T]he military designed basic training as "intensive shock treatment,"
rendering the trainee "helplessly insecure in the bewildering newness
and complexity of his environment."
— Gerald F. Linderman, *The World Within War*

I feel like I'm groping around in an unbaked devil's food cake.
— letter, March 23, 1944

WAR DEPARTMENT
The Adjutant General's Office
Washington

April 30, 1943

Morton Elevitch
1018 Chester Pk. Dr.
Duluth, Minn.

Dear Sir:

It is a pleasure to inform you that you have achieved a satisfactory standing
on the joint Army-Navy qualifying test. Your success on the qualifying test
assures you of special consideration for the Army Specialized Training
Program or the Officer Candidate Schools. You have my best wishes for
your success.

J. A. Ulio, Major General

The Adjutant General

ORIENTATION PAMPHLET
ASTP

The war drain on manpower has depleted college attendance to an extent directly affecting the Army. The steady stream of technically trained men was cut off at its source by the induction of those 18 years old and above, and colleges and universities were emptied to provide replacements for the war program. The Army has recognized this problem. The ASTP was conceived and finally organized as a coordinated system of education at the college level. The Basic Training period will be thirteen weeks, during which the applicant will be trained solely as a soldier in the U.S. Army. Regardless of the trainee's future assignments, duties, schooling, or promotion he is primarily a soldier, first, last and always.

[handwritten on reverse of pamphlet:] We have to put what was formerly a year ½ infantry training into 12 wks, which is supposed to be 13 wks only we got started late here, which means I'll be on Bivouac for 4 wks straight around Christmas which means I'll get mighty, mighty cold and dirty, which means the army is a wonderful thing.

We lay on our beds last night, and talked about the post-war world. Conclusion — we'd just as soon be dead as alive in it. Not my conclusion however.

I'm sitting here with another pimple face, Jack Fanset.

Fort Snelling, Minnesota

October 6, 1943

Dear Mom:

This isn't "the" letter I'll write to you, but I've got some time now so I'll slip this in the day room mail before 0100. Your sandwiches are still reposing quietly in my suitcase. I know that I won't eat them because we get chow very often and very much of it. After we got in here yesterday at 2:25 pm we were given an examination for contagious deseases [*sic*] and then had a blood test. Then we were assigned to rosters (a group of men which goes through Snelling as a unit) and were given bunks. We were shown how to make beds—I got mine right the first time! After chow we were given passes which were good until 12 pm. A kid and I went to see "Watch on the Rhine"—the best picture I've ever seen for 15 cents. Today I was up at 5:30, mopped the floor at 6:30 and had chow at 7:30. Then we were given an orientation talk after which we took a 3-hr series of aptitude tests. This aft we get classified, uniformed and shots. So I'm a very busy lil buck private. So far it's been very interesting. The weather is beootiful. Now I ask you, what have you got to worry about?

October 7

Dear Mable [brother]:

The whole place is clean—and I mean <u>clean</u>. Every private, sergeant or officer I've come into contact with has been o.k. I only hope my training camp is half as good. The man who got this amazing army system going like it is now is really a genius. We got in here at 2:30 Tuesday afternoon. The only thing I remember about our bus ride was (1) a wife telling her husband to come back with "lipstick on your cheek and a star on your shoulder." (My ink is getting low—I've been using my pen a lot.) (2) It was the most beautiful ride I've ever taken. We passed one forest that looked like the Grand Canyon turned inside out. (enter pencil) We were led to barracks and were shown how to make our bunks by our swell roster leader—a Pvt. Dobson. (The next day his wife gave birth to a 6½ lb boy— so he was attending to him instead of us.) The next day our leader was Pvt Hans Hirsch—who talked with a thick German accent. I enjoyed listening to him—especially when he tried to say (huh-thoce) those.

(enter new paper)

For some reason they seem to always rush Duluth men through this place. So immediately we were led off to get our uniforms. First we got two large barrack bags—then underwear, then socks. We went into a room, took off all our civilian clothes for the last time and put on GI stuff. Next I turned a corner and saw men getting their shots. I did <u>not get</u> nervous. I had to watch while a technician got the apparatus ready—and still <u>did not get</u> nervous. He plunged a needle in my right arm. I did not look but on other men I saw the bulge where the needle went in. It stung for 5 seconds and let up just as I got another shot in my left arm. This one, I didn't feel at all. Then we got our shoes. They use a machine to fit you, but I thought mine were too long—as did most everyone. Because the shoes were put on, our arms were kept moving and the injections circulated.

From then on we went down an endless line of "tobacco auctioneers" who measured me and hollered out my sizes. I got more underwear, socks, pants, shirts, ties, hats, jackets, coats, overcoats, caps, fatigue uniforms, canteens, mess kit, towels, handkerchiefs, toothbrush, shaving stuff, leggings, helmet, belt etc. I still haven't found out everything I've got but I never expected to get so much.

At the end I was checked to see if my clothing fit and finally with my packed bag on my shoulder my overcoat over my coat shirt underwear and skin and my helmet on my head I <u>staggered</u> (I mean staggered) out into the hot sun and somehow got to my barrack and bunk. But that was nothing—so I found out today. All the stuff was wrinkled and full of tags—but they look ok.

Today we had a boy ordering us around who called me Eelivitch. I loved him but he meant well.

I sat thru 4 solid hrs of movies on the army and lectures by "Pop the Answer Man" and the chaplain. If every man took their suggestions this would be a utopian army. As it is it is probably much better than a community at home—I mean of course in the way of morals etc., believe it or not. It was good to get outside again and we had chow soon after. I had a half hour to spare so I listened to the world series in the day room.

First thing in the afternoon we wrapped up our civilian clothes, went to the post office and mailed them home. Now the work began—we packed our sheets etc in our bags and lurched for blocks & blocks to the other end of the camp and our shipping co. I was going nuts. (1) The thing was to put it mildly HEAVY! (2) I carried my suitcase in my other hand. (3) My tongue was laying on my shoes—(the tongue from my mouth).

Then we got our dog tags, had chow, and shoved our bags to our huts. Our roster was split up but all in my hut are from Duluth. I was veddy veddy weary.

So here I am in the day room. Harry Von Zell is talking on the "Dinah Shore" program. Tomorrow we start KP duty—or maybe I'll be cleaning the latrine. 4 to 10 days from now I'll be moving to my training camp. I'm in the midst of a great adventure. I will do my best to do my best.

October 13, 1943

Columbus Day

Dear Plasma:

Today I got my first chance to become an expert in goldbricking as we were assigned the woodpile. You are expected to bring, cut up and pile wood. We were situated behind the pile and it soon became evident the task was hopeless, so we sat down. "Hell," said one gentleman reclining on a log, "we're working by preventing this wood from blowing away." Another bent a red leaf, held it to his chest and announced he had received a medal for meritorious duty. "You sat there all your life and grew up with the pile," he was informed. One man worked with tremendous energy but we soon saw he had only made himself a "cave" to sleep in. When our sentries shouted "the corp is coming" you should have seen us work!

October 14

Dear Mom:

This has been a very confusing day. Right now I'm sitting in my OD's (dress uniform) in the Co. 1 Day room. As usual the radio is booming, ping pong balls are placking and billiard balls are clicking. All around is a friendly atmosphere, slightly smoky but nevertheless very condusive to writing. The day was confusing because we moved from our Co. 2 huts at the far end of the camp to the large comfortable two story white barracks of Co. 1. Co. 1 is very strict. Before a person is allowed out of the barracks at night he must shave, wash, shower, brush teeth, comb hair and polish his shoes. Since there are only 8 basins, the 200 men in the barrack really create a problem in the latrine.

This aft I had chow at 3:45 and got ready ahead of most of the others. Before chow we made our beds with clean sheets & pillow cases which would have been OK if we were left alone. However I had to make my bed completely about 6 times because the corporal kept changing his mind as to whether I slept head to the aisle or to the window.

To keep us warm we drilled (I'd rather do this than anything else, surprising as it may seem) for two hours and then played football for two more. For clothing I wear woolen underwear, my thick fatigues, and my soft field jacket. Also we have heavy gloves, so my hands stay warm.

My whole daily schedule has been moved up 2 hrs. I eat breakfast at 6 A.M. Lunch at 11 AM and chow at 4 PM. I've moved my bowels regularly at 5:30 each morning. They say the army is the healthiest place in the world— and I believe it. I haven't even had a headache since I've been down here.

You ought to see the endless lines of civilians moving in here every day. There are many fathers with them. The army certainly shouldn't complain about not getting enough men.

October 18

Dear Omar [brother]:

Friday was my most enjoyable day in the army. After standing and stomping around in lineup for an hour (as usual), I was assigned to the clothing warehouse. I was in pants (I usually am) and handed them out all day. My first duty was to stock up my shelves. With some help I lugged crates of pants to my section, unpacked them and piled them neatly on the shelves. I saw that a crate of 34-33s would not fit in a shelf, so I took out all the original pants and carefully stacked the whole bunch. Some moments later, while swabbing my sweating brow, I was startled to hear a swarthy sergeant sternly shout: "Who put dese here pants in this bin?" (he wasn't too severe when he saw twas me 'cause we were both from Duluth). Anyway I had piled the pants over the 34-33 sign instead of under it. Meekly moving, I threw all the pants in a precarious pile, sorted them out (36-33 from 34-33) and again heaped them up.

All this doesn't sound too thrilling, but soon long lines of timid civilians began filing in. At first I just looked at their size on the slip and quietly handed them two pairs of pants, at the same time telling them to put one on, button up, put on the belt I gave them and put the other pair in the barrack bag. (First they go to measuring—a tobacco auctioneer yells out sizes—then to shirts—then to me).

I began noticing a peculiar chatter going up and down the clothing line (besides the auctioneer). Example: "You say your pants are too small, yer shirts too tight, yer shoes too big, and yer coat too tight? Tell-yuh-whut-ahm gohnna-do . . ."

The guys who were giving out clothing talked to all the civilians, kidded them, cracked jokes, and acted "slightly off." So who was I to be different.

I began by addressing them by their first name (twas on the paper) which surprised them. Once I called a man named Jesse Williams — Jesse James etc. Then I started asking them where they were from, age, married etc. Then I asked them if they'd ever done any dish washing, scrubbing floors or making beds. When they heard enough I reminded them to salute the lewy at the far end of the line (naturally this wasn't necessary). All the time they said "Yes Sir." "Oh you bet Sir." "Thank you, Sir."

They were calling me Sir — and I'd only been in the army 11 days!!

I worked at this all day and Friday eve I went to see "This is the Army" at the State Theater in Mpls. Papa, see it if you can. We got in for 25 cents — you poor civilians have to pay 55 cents but it's worth it.

Last night I saw "Stagedoor Canteen." I wanted to see "The Constant Nymph" but I did not want to wait in line for 30 minutes. By now mom is writhing on the floor. "Oh that child is seeing too many movies. It's bad for him." I used to think it was bad for me too, but I assure you I still am in perfect health anyway.

Today I got a haircut (35 cents). I didn't get a G.I. — maybe later. Around here everyone flips pennies. The reason is that all candy bars, magazines, soap etc. is one or two cents cheaper than in civilian stores. Everytime I'm in the PX I get a few pennies. Oh well every penny counts.

To Burr: Don't take it too hard about Pat's leaving. I understand your feeling for her. It's just one of the heartbreaks in life's long trail. Be brave, ol man.

October 20

[postcard]

Today I was in the guardhouse. But I'm glad I did it — glad I tell you. The squint-eyed sergeant said "Come on, you." Soon I was huddled in a truck with 25 other captives, riding toward my doom. We arrived at last at the tan building with bars on the windows. "Get in there" screamed a musty maverick clutching a .30 rifle. Down a long, gloomy corridor I walked, past slouching men with "Ps" on their backs, scratching their lousy stuble. Then they put me in my cell.

After scrubbing all the woodwork and walls, and shrinking my smarting skin, I got back in the truck and headed back to chow. But I had accomplished something: I'd dusted the chair that Colonel Keeley sits in.

You see, I was in the guardhouse only 10 minutes. The majority of the time I was in the Ft Snelling headquarters. This aft, I was in the Ft Snelling theatre washing windows with Bon Ami. Only about 8 Duluth fellows are left here. Maybe I'll be next.

October 21, 2100

Dear Mom:

I've just (prepare yourself) returned from another movie at the Post theatre — "Girl Crazy" with J Garland, M Rooney, T Dorsey and G Gershwin's music. As I sat there I tryed to imagine Burr's reaction to various things, such as Dorsey's treatment of "Enchantable You," and M Rooney's piano playing, mimicking, acting, singing and dancing.

I went with Al Erickson, and walked back with him. C. Hutchinson, A. Kenner, he and I are the only ones left around here that I really know. Millions of civilians keep coming in here everyday. My barrack has new faces each morning. Pitiful the way they're so ignorant and we veterans have to tell them what to do.

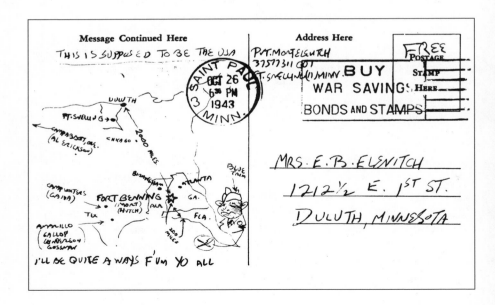

All day today I drilled. I'm glad to get any chance I can to learn some thing because it will be just that much easier when I get to basic. Last nite was the first time I went to bed before 9. It seems like I'm losing something if I go right to bed. I'll have plenty of tired evenings at basic. I just remembered. I was a lead sergeant today. I screamed: "Hut, two hree, fo — ten-hut! — fawd hawsh! raw-it hace!" You can translate it if you try hard.

Now I am going to bed.

Fort Benning, Georgia

October 28, 2030 EST

Dear Burr:

You are the only one I dared write this to in my present state of mind. Maybe when the sun comes up I'll feel different — I don't know. Anyway let no one read this — use your discresion (tion)? about telling of its contents. In short, Snelling was like heaven compared to this. When we first entered in army trucks, after a 14 mile ride from Columbus, the closest town — it looked okay. But we kept going and finally reached a dirty-looking shanty town. Instead of 2 story white barracks with single cots — we found small shacks (no ventilating system) with double beds (one on top of another). I finally got a lower. We get only one sheet — no wonder soldiers get crabs — sleeping under dusty blankets. The only thing good (I think) is the mattress is rather thick. The latrine is not in the barrack but about 7 miles away. It is poorly arranged, poorly lighted and has poor facilities. There is no place to plug in electric razors.

We lined up for chow at 7:30, 10½ hours after our first meal today. We use our mess kits. You file in, they slop stuff in your kit and you walk to a table and eat. Then you stand in line for hours — then move up to a garbage can with boiling water and GI soap in it. You wash (?) out your kit with a brush & then rinse it in boiling water. Naturally I dropped my stuff in the can and scalded my hand. I returned to my barrack I found one kid had a plug — so I unscrewed a light bulb and we used our electric razors to shave. There is no place to hang up your stuff here. The place is heated by a stove. (It gets cold down here now.) By now you see why I wouldn't want anyone to read this but you. I knew the fun at Snelling wouldn't last.

Write at once — I need plenty of cheering up.

October 29, 2015 EST

[to Father]

The boys round here from the South are ok. They do, however, stand firm in their belief in the South's ideals of 1860. We find this silly—but it's no use arguing. I don't mean the ideals are wrong—but I mean the ideas about Negroes and "Yankees." Naturally the guys here from the south mingle with us but they shut up if we mention anything about their customs. One outcome of this war I <u>hope</u> will be an understanding among all peoples in <u>this</u> country. [. . .]

October 30, 1943

Dear—

Well, it's been 4 days at Benning. There are over 140,000 men here altogether, but I've seen the tiny corner of the ASTP camp in which I'm situated. As soon as we get our quota of ASTPs, we'll begin basic training. All my ASTP mates are about my age and come from all parts of the USA. Plenty of southern accents but I like N.Y. accents best. My biggest laugh so far was hearing one guy seriously say: "Afta dis wah ahm gonna be eh radieh eh-noon-sih." . . .

I hope daddy has sent me the electric plug [for electric shaver] I asked for and the tiny flashlight. I also want, now, a chain so I can hang my dog tags 'round my neck—(my cloth one gets too dirty)—

Somewhere off in the distance—guns are being fired—this goes on all day. We do not hear planes here although paratroopers are nearby. All around is a miniature city of blue-green barracks, which blend very well with the azure sky and dark green pines. Below is the reddish sand. Undoubtedly I will never see the whole camp, but I'll feel plenty of it and have most of it on me—All streets have civil war names on them. We have an outdoor auditorium called "Yankee Stadium." How they ever got away with it is a mystery to me.

November 1

[to Burr]

Today we were marched to the big rec halls, where we filled out personal data and ASTP classification sheets. After that we were given a lecture about the ASTP by a very young captain who said among other things that 99% of us would be engineers and that we did not have to sign anything binding our services after the war ended. Then we had an hour long psychological & aptitude test to determine whether or not the reception center had made a mistake in sending us here.

This aft we had our first personal interview. My classifier was very cold and informed me I was to take the 3 battery test tomorrow. If I pass it I'll probably be sent to basic engineering after my 13 wks here. Wish me luck. There was some concern on my part when they learned I had hardly any math or physics and strangely enough that mom and papa were <u>born in foreign countries</u> (????).

Well, so far so good. The good thing about this camp is that it's already a so-called "star" unit, and before you begin training you know whether your in ASTP or not.

Chow is quite a hullaballoo. You cannot leave to get more or wash your equip until <u>everything</u> is eaten (we're inspected). At the table there are certain procedures to follow, short stopping is intolerable. If a man asks for the sugar or the butter you're supposed to pass it right to him and not help yourself. Also, in order to get it next, you must yell "Butts on that!" After eating, we file out and clean (?) our messkits in barrels of soapy boiling water. Am I eating dirt now!

The shower is another hullaballoo. About 600 guys all crowd into one place. In the shower it was OK. But outside: My clean underwear was on the wet floor. My shoes containing my dog chain [*sic*] and watch were separated. Piles of clothing—all looking alike are littering the benches. What a mess!

One Brooklynite here has studied Japanese for 2 yrs. at Columbia. He was one of the very few to get in the language division. They call him "Ash-kan."

I like to listen to the New Yorkers talk better than the Southerners.

November 2

... We went to take our 3 hr IQ mechanical and signal corps test. I later learned that I had made enough in the IQ test (over 115) to still be eligible for ASTP. In the mech. I had decided mech. ability—read that again dad. Now get off the floor and read it again. The man had his eyes squinting and his nose an inch away from the paper when he wrote. He found out everything about everything I've ever done. He asked me what type of cartooning I'd done, how long and for whom, what characters I've played on the radio, he said "anyone can write—not many can cartoon" ...

November 3

Dear Capsule:

I'm counting on you again to soften papa and mom in case they inform me tomorrow that I don't have the proper background for ASTP. Anyway we have our final interview tomorrow. Our basic training will be over Feb. 1, 1944, so you can figure that in March I'll either be in some college as an engineering student, or overseas with the infantry.

Halloween night two men entered our barrack—one with a blue trimmed infantry cap and one with the formerly termed "garrison hats" now "service hats." They went around to each bed with a flashlight, asking who was on K.P. the next day. Dave Elkins pipes up: "What time is it, bub?" "WHAT??—get out of bed—don't you know you can't talk to the cadre like that? What's your name?" "Pvt. Basic—what's yours?" Anyway, it was two pvts from the 6th Co. posing as cadremen. Three of our boys chased them out of the hut, caught them and gave them a G.I. bath. (If you want any more info as to what a G.I. bath is I'll send you details upon request.) "Cadre" is French for instructor. I think.—they're all Cpls, Sgts, etc.

Today we had the afternoon to scrub our huts after our tests this morn. As soon as I get back in my barrack we are called out for formation. It seems that my hut 127 and 126 had too many beds made unright—so we had a special detail. I marched thru clouds of sand and then lugged and set up tables and chairs in a rec hall. Just then I find my dog tags are not wagging around my neck. This is the last straw—I misplaced them somewhere. Besides, I am all dirty. Besides, I am worried about the outcome of my test. Besides, I don't want KP Sunday. Besides, I am tired.

Tonight, as last night, I had a pint of ice cream to eat. It is 20 cents but it's the closest thing to milk even though it's made with water. They have the biggest rackets here—PX that charges the same or more for stuff civilians can buy. Barber shop that changes 40 cents for a 5 minute haircut. I am now spending lots of money.

As usual we had a mail call. As usual my name wasn't mentioned. As usual all my friends from North Dakota were. As usual I went away wondering if you were still laying around after celebrating my leaving. This may seem unusual but I want a letter from someone every day. Mostly you. I also want a steel dog tag chain. They have to be made especially for dog tags.

By the way, I found my yappers 3 hrs later laying behind a foot locker in my barrack.

Nov. 2nd I was very miserable. I could not move my bowels. Twas the first time since 1937.

I went to the dispensary and a med tech gave me some black stuff to drink. I told him about my meat situation, and how my bowels have been affected since I've been eating meat. He advised me to <u>lay off meat</u> if I wanted to. I was very much surprised at what he said—but I notice many guys here pass up meat too.

Everyone's singing "Take Down Your Service Flag, Mother, Your Son's in the ASTP." Don't know whether you can sing it or not. The test was: 85 questions on Science-Human Body, Astronomy, Biology, Physics, 79 on math—mostly geom—solid, alg, and trig. Then we had stuff in which we had to read a paragraph or look at diagrams or graphs and answer questions about them. Very confusing when you know you have to hurry and your future depends on it.

Enough babble. Goodbye. I'm getting used to it here—Tso kay.

Coolidge

November 4

THE INTERVIEW

I sat around with 300 fellows—almost—outside the rec hall. They kept calling out names and lining up guys but not me. As the afternoon wore on perspiration began trickling down my face as I realized "they were saving us flunks for the last." The longer I waited, the more I worried, and the more I worried, the worse I felt. How would I tell you I wondered—how <u>could</u> I tell you. I had already thought up the telegram: ASTP ACCEPTED ME STARTING BASIC ENGINEERING FRIDAY—but I knew it wouldn't be sent.

Finally there were only 25 of us left. With our tongues hanging out we slobbered about the tiny corporal as he wheezed out our names. "Eleeevish"—he bellowed. "Here" I coughed as I staggered toward the line. I had waited 3 hrs. Before I went in I knew I had been accepted. A man at the door told us all the rejects had went in first—so I was calm when it was time for my interview. The captain didn't say much accept that I was to be put in term one of basic engineering—he asked if I wanted to go to school (silly man) and wondered if I had any questions. I found out that I had a mark of 95 for my phys-geom test (60 was passing). This however is not good—there are over 150 questions in the test. Only 6 who came here got rejected.

Well here's my opportunity. Maybe I'll make good. At least, I'll be in school 3 months.

This is in the latest "Yank" — I tried to get a CDD; instead they gave me ASTP. P.S. T.S. (For your information CDD is Certificate of Doctor's Discharge. TS is tough shit.)

"Take Down Your Service Flag, Mother, Your Son's in the ASTP" has 50 verses — In the chorus is "Goldbrick — Goldbrick — we're all in the ASTP." 49 of the 50 verses are unprintable.

Tomorrow I'm on latrine orderly until noon when our basic training gets off to a flying start.

November 14, 1943. "Right after chow, to make sure we were thoroughly warmed up and had no kinks, we had rifle cal in the hot sun. Bare except for pants. Now rifle calisthenics is vastly different from regular cal. Besides supporting your head and legs and arms you must swing a bulky rifle around—I'm not kidding when I say it nearly pulls your arms out of your sockets. How we sweated. Rifle cal is a preview to bayonet exercises which we'll have this week."

November 9, 2120

Dear Barney:

I'm writing this atop my bunk before I turn in after my 2nd day of basic.
This eve I had a G.I. haircut finally (because I was strongly urged to by the
Sarg this morn). I think I look better in it than I did before.

[. . .] Because I was a latrine orderly, I missed my first half day of
basic—(instruction on M-1 rifle) . . in the afternoon we saw an hour movie
on: "Why we're fighting the war." Then one on chemical warfare. During
the lecture "sniffing bottles" were passed about containing mustard,
chlorine, adamsite, Lewisite and phosgene gases. Soon much coughing
and sneezing. My nose still smarts. These talks aren't given in one place.
Between each one we'd march in formation to a different place, but all of
them were given in outdoor amphitheaters under the pines.

After that we got our blankets and packs and I learned how to make
them up. The "gig" system began operating. If during inspection a person
or his belongings or bed are found out of order or not "GI" he is gigged
and gets KP on Sunday or more undesirable jobs. 8 "gigs" and a person is

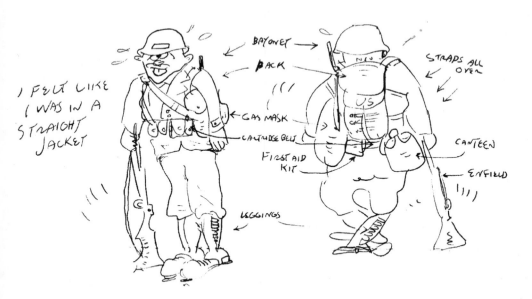

restricted to his barrack for as long as the M Sarg decides. We also have a dummy squad which drills at night. These fellows are the ones who during the day move at inspection, talk in line etc. Things are getting tough.

The other day I took a walk up to the "big PX" located in the 4th regiment which is about 8 blks over the hill. It was just like coming into a big city. Here the barracks are two story and white and there is grass and trees around them. The 4th regiment ASTP lives in the residential district of Fort Benning whereas we live in the slums. Oh well we have much more fun with small barracks—and it's more like the "written about" army life. I just looked at a sign on our door which originally said "This building burns in 15 minutes." Only now it says "This building was built in 15 minutes."

November 10, 2055

Dear Wuk—

You think you are having tough time learning some things. Ha! I giggle with extraordinary glee. This basic training she is not something for dumbbell to bouncing on his brain. Oh no. Already three days it is being for me. First thing, of course, we are getting up—that is, as usual being official waker upper of my barrack 127 am doing the dirty work by turning on lights. Chow she is eatable. We along take cartridge belt packs and rifles. Then we stack rifles after marching long. My gun is always knocking against side of my helmet tilting it most uncomfortable over my eye and ear also, but I am marching at attention so I rectify it cannot. The Lt who looks like Walter Brennan told us a joke about girl who running thru burning woods. She is picking up fleeing monkey. Finally she is surrounded by fire. "Well I guess I'm screwed," she says. "Can't help it lady—it's the only way I can hold on," says monkey.

By the way I am stack man or key man in "stack arms." Then we see how pitch tent. Lectures we had on military post and guard duty, military marches and the gas mask—then we put on our gas masks in a prescribed way. The Lt (talks like J Cagney) really gave it to us fast. When I got mine on I nearly suffocated until I stopped gripping the tube.

STRAPS ALL OVER

November 14, 1855

Dear Mom:

Now that I'm here I'm satisfied. Already I have made friends and have
a feeling of companionship. I've never had it before. They call me
"Minnesota" because most of us can remember the state rather than the
name. Tonite I took a shower and shampoo. The way my hair is cut makes
shampoo easy. Also a GI is more comfortable. I think I may keep a GI
haircut even after I get in college. I was at the PX and saw a Negro in a
genuine zoot suit: Wow! What a blaze of color!

November 14, 1943

Garbled Information (I)

Mom wants to know "where they'll send me" . . I don't know—but I'll
be going with my hut mates. One of them, Lawrence Falstein, the gazelle-
necked lad in my barrack—is just getting over his poison ivy, but he has
not washed his neck in over a week, and resembles a wood pecker peeking
out of a stovepipe.

It was a good thing Burr's letter came Friday. I had just completed a very
distressing day. I was "Mohr-toning" all over the place. My helmet was too
big for me. When I ran it either came off or rattled around on my head.
When I snapped my cranium to the side and front in "count off" it usually
ended up over my right ear. Naturally at attention I couldn't straighten it
out—because a worse offense is to move. Once while marching, Lt. Toop
said: "Straighten your helmet, Elevitch"—but I couldn't keep it straight—
because my '17 rifle kept scraping it when it bounced up and down on my
shoulder . . . Yesterday I loosened all the straps so my head will go in farther.

Saturday was exactly opposite from the day before. I thought it would
start out bad, though, because we put on all our equipment and started on
a long march. When we're given "Route-step-marsh" we can talk, sing, etc
so it proved to be a lot of fun. But soon we started filing uphill thru the
woods . . We halted on a high hill, were told this was a practice bivouac
and to disperse and pitch our tents . . . easy on the parade grounds, but
here we had many things to contend with. The tent stakes wouldn't hold,
the ground was covered with sticky vines etc., but we got ours up, covered
it with branches and leaves to camouflage it. Lt. Toop criticized our work.
The main thing was our tents were too close together (a 50 mortar shell
could wipe out 30 of us at once) and some kids pointed theirs uphill, which

would have allowed rain to pour in. This adventure was very instructive.

On the way back we passed the eighth company and exaggerated the horrible ordeal they were about to go thru. For the record I'll mention all the cadremen here are of the best, since most of them were flunked out of ocs (Officer Candidate School) in the last week. The co-commander is Capt Herron, Lts are Toop, Chew, Bullock and Young. My Sgt is Anderson; Cpls are Pelletier and Robbins.

The privates in my hut have been editors of publications in high school, or in music . . They can all act (in a way) and can sing—so you see my evenings aren't too dull.

I am the 2nd man in the 3rd squad of the 1st platoon of the 7th company of the 2nd Battalion of the 5th Training Regiment of ASTP.

I am not kidding when I say we get exercise. After the long hike Saturday we had foot inspection . . Then we had drilling—doubletime. Then, just before lunch, we had calisthenics. Then we doubletimed back to our stacks, put on all our equipment and doubletimed back to our area. (This isn't meant to make you feel sorry for me—you should feel good because I can take it) . . .

I really would have liked to have seen that snow. I'm sorry to hear about daddy's man (or woman) problem [help for his store]—Uncle Sam has quite a plentiful supply here: Fort Benning has an area of 660 miles.

The platoon commanders keep charts of every man and mark us . . . If a person gets a "U" in anything he won't go to ASTP—so I'll have to put college out of my mind and concentrate on being a good soldier. Affectionately, Uncle Freddy.

Forgot to mention we have Italian pws here—they planted oats that's right oats right in front of our huts!

November 14, 1943

[To Brother]

Garbled Information (II)

You'd be surprised at the food wasted here. I had to throw away gallons of perfectly good scrambled eggs and bisquits. The mess sergeant really kept "on our ass" (army lingo). We carried boxes of chickens, meat, fruit, etc. We scrubbed, cleaned, wiped and piled.

The night before we got off early because we were relieved by extra duty men. All guys gigged are put in the kitchen and work until 11:30 PM. "Star gigs" get Sunday K.P. I've been gigged three times—for forgetting my belt, for being slow at manual of arms (I had my gloves in one hand)—for dropping my rifle. As yet I havent got extra duty—but as I write this I expect the serg to come in and break the news. Gigs are given if a man's finger sticks up in manual, for being unshaven, or helmets tipped, buttons unbuttoned etc. A GUN IS NOT A GUN IN THE ARMY IT'S AN M-1, A '17 OR MAYBE A RIFLE. They gig us if we forget.

We KPS got chow to the men 5 miles from camp—in the woods. Then we listened to lectures on anti-tank mines, grenades, BAZOOKA (saw one) etc. We learned about and did camoflage. Noncoms camoflaged themselves in gunny sacks, leaves etc and we tried to find them. Twas fun. After we hid ourselves and were criticized. Next we laid flat and dug slit trenches. Just lie flat on the floor and you can imagine how it is to quickly dig a hole with a bayonet.

The next lecture was on observing the enemy. We took concealment 50 yds from the crest of a hill and slowly crawled forward to our lookout positions. All this time understand I had MY THUMB OVER THE MUZZLE to keep the dirt out. Then we were ready for "Hell's Half Acre," a 300 yd stretch of ground covered with everything to get a person dirty, scratched, bruised, and miserable. Officers were dispersed about. If we lifted our head, they BASHED IT WITH A RIFLE. If we lifted our heels they STAMPED ON THEM. This was the real thing at last. No one touched me. I SAW TO THAT.

2220. This, I emphasize is not intended to make you feel sorry for us. We all appreciate and respect our officers because they are doing things to protect our lives in case we ever get into battle. We all know our officers & cadremen are the cream of the crop. They know what they're doing so we don't gripe (much). Our feet are continually inspected.

Next day they had the gas chamber prepared for us. It was just a tent full of nice tear gas. All we had to do was enter with our gas masks, remove the masks inside, grope around until they let us out. Harder to do was: Enter tent minus gas mask and DON MASK IN DARKENED CROWDED INTERIOR OF TENT. At first the gas just burns a bit. Outside: TEARS START STREAMING OUT OF YOUR RED, SMARTING, BLOOD-SHOT EYES. This was intended to show us the value of our gas masks. It did.

1520. Since talking to you this morning I've rode the bus to Columbus with Ellicott & Fanset and here I am in one of the Service Centers overlooking the main street of the town. It really will be nice if I am able to get here every week. Everything I could desire is here except Duluth.

2045. I'm now back in my barrack. I'm hungry—all I had since 1520 was an egg sandwich, another quart of milk, a bag of potato chips, a chocolate ice cream cone, some orange punch, piece of cake, a handful of peanuts and a cookie. Oh yes—a pkge of cheese crackers and peanut butter.

Friday morning we packed a full field pack, consisting of tent, tent poles, stakes, rope, a blanket, a raincoat, extra socks, and a mess kit. With this on our backs for the first time, it was easy to understand why a soldier has a straight back.

The officers informed us we were going on a 9 mile hike to a bivouac area where we were to pitch tents. Being in the 2nd file of the 3rd squad of the 1st platoon of the 7th co. puts me in an excellent position. On marches I'm always at the very front of the long, long column of soldiers. This eliminates a lot of dust eating—and I don't have to run every few steps to keep "closed up." After an hour we had a rest, and they made us TAKE OFF OUR SHOES AND STOCKINGS. AGAIN OUR FEET WERE CLOSELY SCRUTINIZED.

I had trouble keeping in step because the officers never bothered to do same. When we reached the top of a hill I glanced back and saw our column trailing for blocks behind all in perfect cadence—made an impressing sight. The morning was suited for a hike—cool, crisp and exactly as 99% of Georgia mornings have been. The landscape dotted with pines seemed to shimmer as our shadows weaved beside the highway. We passed numerous training areas, set aside for tactics and mortar practice. Finally we reached a beautiful Georgia forest, and deep in its innards we came to a halt. Immediately we were formed in squads and disregarding the tangled growths, we plunged into the designated area and proceeded to pitch our tents. We camoflaged them with everything under the sun. In fact we did such a good job the captain came to our territory and started swearing because he thought we were late. When a head popped out he nearly collapsed.

Then we were the first platoon to repack and get ready for marching. I picked up some long pine needles and stuck them in my helmet to send you. Notice their length—and you will understand why seeing 100,000 of them in thousands of trees is a sight to behold.

All the way back we again saw lakes and streams, reminding me of Minnesota. The leaves here are just turning red and as far as I'm concerned, we couldnt have hiked in a better place. We started singing various songs. We screamed ourselves hoarse and the Lt never turned around but I saw the creases in his jaw:

> "The 1st Platoon is the best of all / Inky dinky parly voo
> Because theyre always on the ball / Inky dinky parly voo
> The 2nd Platoon is in a rutt / they're always sitting on their butt
> The 3rd Platoon is out of our class / They've all got bullets up their—
> The 4th platoon's the goon platoon . . ."

Back at camp at 12:20 we had our feet and backs inspected. The funniest feeling I've ever had took place after I removed my pack. In trying to walk I seemed to spring up and down like a kangaroo.

Every muscle in my body was howling by 2000 Friday And they-en and they-en I HAD GUARD DUTY Friday night! Interior guard is the most serious ceremony in the army—the responsibility put on a sentinel is tremendous. They pound in to us the importance of security. We all had to be as beautiful as possible so I put on all fresh clothes, including OD [olive drab] pants and shirt I've never worn. In 45 minutes we had to eat, get dressed, washed and clean our sandy rifles—the 40 of us did some fancy hustling. The ceremony connected is very formal but we were at attention without moving our eyeballs for more minutes then I care to mention.

I was lucky again. It was not very light when the OD [officer of the day] inspected us so he didnt notice my spotted and dirty jacket. He inspects rifles by grabbing it. You are then supposed to drop your arms. This is not as easy as it sounds. Some don't let go.

Still lucky I had post No 5 from 7 to 9 PM. Nothing much happened except someone did some "promiscuous pissing" on my post. It really was an experience pacing up and down with a gun on my shoulder—I had supreme authority on my post and had to see to it that everything was in order. Under the stars (no moon) I can see why guard duty can be very lonely. But at this hour I could hear a jam session in progress in the rec hall. I honestly hated to be relieved—Slong

THE EPIC OF FALSTEIN

Once upon a midnight dreary
When in bed we were quite weary
And the rain began to pour
As thunder shook us with a roar
There was Falstein pissing, pissing
Slowly pissing out the hutment door.

Drowzy Drescher in his bed
Raised upright his sleepy head
Intently listened for a snore
Heard what he'd not heard before
Falstein pissing, pissing
Slowly pissing out the hutment door.

And when the incident was done
We covered up one by one
Smiled a bit and smiled some more
Not a one of us was sore
About Falstein pissing, pissing
Slowly pissing out the hutment door.

[Author unknown]

November 22, 2015

Dear Mater:

After I called Sunday, Fanset, Ellicott, Falstein and I left for Columbus. The fare is 15 cents and we rode on a peculiar bus—resembling a transport truck crossed by a Greyhound bus. It takes about half an hour to get to the town, and the ride is worth 15 cents. The scenery is really gorgeous now, since the leaves are turning red. When first entering Columbus, all you see is dingy dilapidated houses occupied by Negroes. They are all built up on columns—having no basements whatsoever. The Negroes all sit on their front porches eating, talking or sleeping. Any person liking character study would have appreciated seeing the Negro section of Columbus.

We walked up and down the entire main street looking for open military stores, but since it was Sunday, only two were open. I bought a snazzy blue braid infantry cap ($1.95). Altogether I only spent around 4 dollars all day.

I got tired saluting—as the town was crowded with officers. By 5 PM we had seen all of Columbus we cared to for the time being, and decided to go to the Main Post. Just before reaching it we passed more Negro sections. What a contrast! The main post is beautiful! IT LOOKED EXACTLY LIKE A COLLEGE CAMPUS TOWN.

I saw a magnificent red brick structure, outstanding in architectural design. I found out it was THE GUARDHOUSE!

The officers' pools clubs and homes are so stunning it left me breathless, all alike—cream in color, with jade green trimmings, red Spanish tile roofs and black scotties that yap just like typical city dogs.

Got back at 8:30 after my most enjoyable day in three wks.

Slong

By gosh I still have half an hour—so I'll go ahead. We saw the third of seven remarkable pictures on "why we are fighting the war." I saw another movie Saturday night. There was a singing reel—when it said "Girls sing" we all screamed the words in shrill voices. Wery [sic] mucho fun.

Yesterday they took us out in a swamp. THEN THE BLASTED CADREMEN ran away AND WE HAD TO FIND OUR WAY BACK ALONE. Some fun. At least the training program doesn't get boring—we do something different every day.

I haven't said this for a long long time but you know I love you and in spite of my aloof letters—I still try to take you in my complete confidence—

November 23, 2045

Dear Louisa:

For the Nth time, thanks for your package. Please don't send me any more underwear, socks, or candy. The Milk of Magnesia was absolutely unnecesary—I'M HAVING NO MORE BOWEL TROUBLE AND DON'T ANTICIPATE ANY.

This week they are teaching us to kill. Now you probably looked away and shuttered. Well, mom, I don't like the idea, either, but we all know it's for our own good. The most strenuous work we do takes place as we stand in one place—bayonet drill. We lunge about in definite movements and are required to growl, grimace, and look at each other with hate. Five hundred of us dance about, screaming, shouting and snarling. A rifle seems to weigh a ton more with a bayonet on. Our arms feel as if they're going to drop off as the Lt holds us in one position and talks! Our bayonets have sheaths on them so that no one has his head cut off. They teach us how to withdraw our bayonets in a certain manner, too, because steel sticks to warm human flesh. (This sounds awful bloodthirsty but everyone keeps serious minded about it.)

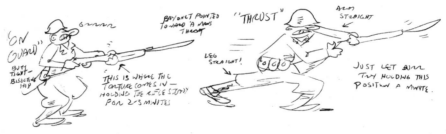

We are also learning jiu jitsu holds—and to put it bluntly—plain dirty fighting. This will be invaluable in case anyone ever tries to pick on me. Maybe I shouldn't put this in—in fact I know I shouldn't—but it is going on so—Our instructors emphasize that we should be quick or be dead—always try to kill a man—break his arm first—then clip him under the nose—throat, neck or kidneys to kill him.

I'm afraid I'll never be an expert at this, because I just can't bring myself to go at this in earnest. Surprize is a very important element—I know how to break any hold, grip and throw a man flat on his face—They even teach us how to scientifically stomp on a man. I've left out many gory details.

By the way everything is done in double time this week. We move in place and from place to place on the double—puff puff.

Confidentially, I'm tired.

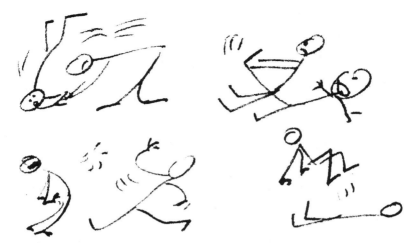

"We are also learning jiu jitsu — and plain dirty fighting" (figures much enlarged from original letter).

November 27, 1943

Dear Walburn:

Last night I saw "Thousands Cheer" in technicolor. I could just imagine as I sat there — Burr "Burring" all over the place when Jose Iturbi directed the orchestra. I wish Burr could see it and "Burr" to me about it. By the way, Burr, Lena Horne appears in it. Yesterday I saw about 4 movies altogether.

November 29, 1943

Dear Tokum:

All afternoon we marched and marched and marched — with full field packs! All the way back I kept up a continual chatter — driving everybody nuts. I went thru the entire Homer in Hudson routine. Then I started telling stories — which I made up as I went along. Back again I was plenty hoarse, but I hardly noticed the miles pass by — and I felt fresher than when I started. After this I talk all the way.

Hikes are beginning to take their toll. One guy fainted today — another just sat down and would go no further. Both got lifts in the colonel's jeep. We saw new territory this aft — hundreds of trees with deep maroon leaves. My feet are taking punishment but they're o.k. I sprinkle mom's powder on them — at night whether it does good or not. Hon horrors! Tomorrow night we have a night problem.

December 2, 1943

Dear Babli:

I want to impress you that it is cold down here. The lowest temperature was 12 above—but this cold is moist-damp-penetrating—It actually snowed—real determined-like all morning—Boy, I liked the looks of the cool white flakes. Last night in town I spent $11.00. With my friends Fanset and Ellicott I ran into every store and finally sent you another package. I came in early because I wanted to rest up for guard duty tonight—Humor: Toop gives "to the rear march," Della-Rose doesnt hear it, keeps marching straight ahead, soon discovers his error—comes pounding back. Toop gives "to the rear march," Della-Rose screeches to a stop—bowling over the whole front of our column as they turn around—S long

December 3, 1943

I got paid again—$24.85—Yesterday we got a chance to dig foxholes, mortar emplacements and machine gun nests. The fox holes (two men dig in an hour) are 3½ 2 feet in dimensions and deep enough so you can peer over the edge. One guy had his camouflaged with a pine needle lid—Twas so good he fell in it and sprained his ankle. By the time we finish our little home it has everything but running water. Everyone gets disgusted as he finishes his emplacements, starts to rest, and hears a yell: "Fill in and prepare to move out." I found out it's more work to fill in the hole than to dig it. . . Usually we have an hour of hand-to-hand a day—Now I can disarm a man charging me with a knife! A whole bunch of rookies came in today . . Only 59 more days to go!

December 7, 1943

Dear Leotard:

Oh, oh, it's late . . Today we learned about and built barbed wire emplacements and—had a forced march—We RAN with <u>full</u> field packs— Okay, faint mom.

Yesterday morning we ran the grenade course, crawling up to trenches, mach gun nests, craters, etc. Lt Tyler was up on a balancing bar watching us; a grenade flew thru the air, smacked his foot: broken foot. The afternoon was soothing. For four hours we studied the machine gun, learning the names, dissembling, assembling, functioning and care of its parts.

Then we had a night problem. It was really pouring. Lined up for three miles were over 100 cadremen armed with machine guns, rifles, blank ammunition, flares, and—flour bombs. If they heard the slightest noise they fired, threw flares—and usually crept up and covered us with flour— Anyway, the whole show was run wrong—the patrols were sent out at too short intervals—it wasnt long before all the patrols were separated and were following the wrong leaders—I was on my own in ten minutes. If we were caught by the enemy we had to clean their wet guns (that night), go over the course again and worst of all—get a "u" for the night problem. I turn my head—spit out some weeds and see two feet two inches away. The other guys "ran like hell"—exactly the opposite from what we'd been taught. So I gets caught and they dont. Anyway I keep going after the guy takes my name. I had Ashkenas' rifle—since he had a compass and my rifle had no sling. What a nightmare! I rolled over a hill, caught the sling and me in a vine and nearly wreck us. We cross a stream. I stept in and filled my shoes with water. For hours afterward I could feel the rise and fall of the tide.

I finally got the flour. Soon I was covered with regular paste (flour and water variety) hindering my progress immeasurably. By 11 PM I had no idea where I was—at 11:10 I was confronted with flashlights. They told me I was through. Lt Toop informed me THAT I WAS THE FIRST IN MY PATROL. I told him I was caught. He said not to worry, everyone but one had been—"GO GET SOME HOT COFFEE AND GO TO BED"—(no cleaning of rifles?)—As it was I got hot milk and rolled in bed by 11:30. I slept and in the morning wasnt sick.—I guess I must be an individualist.

December 14, 1943

Dear Mizmo:

Did I ever tell you my most valuable article of G.I. clothing? It's my good old helmet—it keeps rain off my head, I use it for a pillow during "breaks." I can sleep thru lectures since its low visor shades my eyes from the sun & Lt Toop—But more important it guards my head from the sharp low rafters in our hut. It hides stuff put under it during inspection. It can be used for a football.

My friend Fanset went to Atlanta over the wk end with the ASTP chorus. He heard Nathan Milstein at a concert. Only 47 days to go! Keep smilin

December 19, 1943

Dear Veneer:

All this week we concentrated on learning the operation, functions, sighting, aiming, firing, assembling, dissembling, mounting the morter, machine gun and M1 rifle. Of all these weapons, I think I'd rather be a mortarman [later called "Mortar Mort"].

Everything is done with precision and polish—making a snappy and interesting effect when 500 men do every little movement at the same time. The captain said our company did the best in machine gun and rifle instruction and also on guard. Our co. is getting a reputation of being the best in the regiment. The whole idea is to make sharpshooter on the M-1 and now I can wear <u>two</u> medals on my chest!

December 24

Dear Pathic—

Christmas eve—tonight I shaved with a safety razor for the first time in my life! I won't be able to call you next Sunday as I've intended—we'll all be 18 miles away on bivouac—two solid weeks.

0930. G'mornin. Christmas morn. I'm sitting on a footlocker wearing the fatigue coveralls I bought and mom's sleeveless sweater. It's warm in here. A big, red paper bell hangs from a rafter swinging in the heat from the stove below it. Draped around it are fatigues, underwear and socks, still damp from last night's washing. The radio is on low. Only two lights are showing—outlining the stirring bodies rolled up in bed. Outside the weather is great—just about freezing—windy—and rain rushing down as if pulled by a powerful magnet. Goelke sits beside me head in his hands. I said "What's the matter, Ken?" He didn't answer. You should see the floor. Field packs, shoes, towels, leggings, canteens, bags, bottles, cans, socks, paper, boxes, candy wrappers, string all over the floor. But enough of this sentiment.

The range we went to yesterday is only 2½ miles away but wearing over-coats is very hampering. Our co. had the pits in the morning and was scheduled to fire in the afternoon. Work in the pits was hard but exciting. Here is the picture: The firers were on perfectly level land—surrounded by hills and trees. The targets came up over a high dirt ridge—reinforced by timbers & sand bags—behind which—were the pits. Farther on was a whole forest resembling gnawed toothpicks—thousands of 30 caliber bullets having whittled the trees down. The target was mounted in a moveable frame before us—connected to pulleys and weights. The target was made of paper mounted on canvas and was 6 ft square.

Our routine for 5 hrs went something like this: up the range—the speaker would blare—"Ready on the right.—Ready on the left"—then over the telephone to our pits—"ready on the firing line." A noncom would caution us with "The flag is up. The flag is waving—The flag is down— 5 seconds—targets—UP!"

At once we'd give a terrific tug on a rope and 50 targets would go shooting up above us to face the blazing barrels. We'd crouch back in our pits and soon hear the whip and whang of bullets over our heads. Once in a while we'd hear a "wup" sounding like popping popcorn—and we'd know that our target had been hit. Some bullets would ricochet off sandbags or the wooden frames, sending sand and splinters cascading before us.

After 40 seconds of the din—the noncoms would scream—Targets— down!! Again we'd grab that rope and yank down our target—immediately we took markers—black or white cards with pegs in them—and stuck them in bullet holes—white on the bull—and black elsewhere. This marked the target—showing the shooter where he hit. When the target went up again we had to give the firer his score. This was done by poking up long steel poles with different colored round markers on the ends— denoting various points—a red flag for a "Maggie's drawers" or 0.

Down went the targets again—One guy pulled out the markers, another put paste from a pot over and around the holes and still another (usually me) pulled apart tiny perforated paper squares and jabbed them over the holes. Every pit along the line tried to outdo the others by hollering "Up" first. Pretty soon—up they flew—good as new—and we'd crouch back again—hearts beating—waiting for the whine of the bullets.

Another thing we had to do was to make sure the target was centered and in the frame. It would have been the end of us if our target got blown off across the range. The wind blew the markers off time and time again— forcing us to crawl around underneath the catwalk and find them.

Were we rushed around noon! The 8th Co. was allowed "alibi" runs for jammed rifles etc, necessitating more "targets up" and much more time taken—so by 12:30 we had to hurry like demons to get thru. It was unbelieveable that we could do all those things so fast without getting in each other's way but we did—The noncoms would yell ready 8? ready 9?

ready 10 — ready 11 etc and threaten us with KP if we slowed up. Then targets up! and another mad cycle. OF ALL WORKING JOBS I'VE HAD IN THE ARMY — I ENJOYED THIS THE MOST.

Twas a good thing they had a good chow! — Everybody was starved at 1:30 . . .

Now it was our turn to fire. By the way, in case I haven't mentioned it we used 30 cal carbine rifles. As you know I had never fired a rifle in my life. I was on target 48 with 4 other guys.

Using "Tennessee aiming" due to the wind — I, as most fellows, didn't do so well. My grand total was 121 out of 160 — this was not firing for the record — that comes next week — so I did okay. The kick was very slight — I'd point the thing at the target — hoping I was aiming and holding it right — pretty soon it exploded and I'd see the muzzle wave way off the target — Maggie's drawers I'd think to myself — By god — the target would come up with <u>white</u> markers on it !! [bull's-eyes] Never will be able to figure it out.

December 24

This morning I got up at 9:30 — (OH WHAT A NIGHT!) Washed with a clean towel — got Ellicott up — walked out into a clear — cold — bright morning! Had breakfast — (2 waffles, qt of milk (to eat more doughnuts with) ($1.25 for both of us) Now I'm at the USO — I am going back real early to (1) get cleaned up and shaved for the last time in 2 wks — (2) put my stuff away — (3) Rest (4) Roll my pack — All our necessities for the two weeks will be carried in the packs — we dont take barrack bags this time (!) In the packs — my shelter half — blanket — raincoat — toilet articles — underwear — socks and handkerchiefs — Tied to the outside will be comforter — other blanket and overcoat — OHMIGOT — We gotta hike with all that — I leave Monday at 8 AM — We'll have two wks of night problems and maneuvers — Do not expect a word from me for 2 wks!

You write to me — Try to get the Jan 12 Colliers — Excellent Damon Runyon story in it —

Sunday Dec. 26

18 miles of mud! — the backs of our shoes, leggings, and pants were getting mud packs until soon we had to walk stiff-legged. The next thing that bothered me was the steel helmet. I didn't mind it was so heavy — but it bounced up and down — at the same time the strap kept slapping me in

the face—It had a regular cadence—hut-two-three-four—slap in the nose—slap in the mouth—slap on the chin—slap in the neck—I happily convinced myself that I wasn't even tired and resolved to put my "unnoticeable mile" method into effect. So for the next few miles—walking beside Fanset—I related the story of the "Two Blue Gnus and the Yak that lived in a Red Brick Bungalow Reinforced with Portland Cement and the various other articles which can be accumulated from the High Hills Steep Ridges and Deep Valleys of the Himalaya Mts"—which I made up as we squished along. Before I knew it we had a break and it was time to eat—contrary to what I'd heard the "C" rations were remarkably good and the contents of the 2 × 3 cans were very filling because of the concentration—

Only 5 miles to go—We passed many rifle, mortar and machine gun ranges—The last one only 1 mile from camp. Here Capn Herron stood with extended forefinger denoting the distance left. Staggering into the tent city we passed the 5th and 6th Cos who arrived first and were greeted very hospitably with "What's this—sick call?"

.. In the army we are supposed to (in the words of Lt Young) grab a man's balls, pull them down to his knees, and let them riquochet off his legs. After that we break his arms or legs, pop his eardrums, gouge out his eyes, smack him in the nose, throat, neck, and kidneys and stomp on him. If he isnt dead yet, we just use our bayonet on him. Well—I'm leepy. G'night

January 9, 1944

Dear Moosh:

Been back in civilization four hours now. YOU CANT IMAGINE HOW A HOT SHOWER AND SHAMPOO FEELS AFTER NOT HAVING ONE FOR FIFTEEN DAYS —this morning at 5:20 AM . . . prepared for another 18 mile trek thru the mud (ten inches deeper by now). The sergeant he is saying—Elevi-tich— you is on baggage detail—No—this cant be I am pleading on bended knees but the sergeant insists so I shut up—This means I cant walk the 18 miles— all I do is merely help throw 250 light barrack bags on trucks—The reason I begged to walk with my platoon is obvious—me riding—them walking— Leaves a bad taste in my mouth—but I had a roaring fire waiting for them and the fact is nobody said a word about it—except my feet—they annoy me—smirking all the time—

TUESDAY—Fired the mortar—I was the gunner (he adjusts the sights— cranks—turns—yells "Fire") when the no. 2 man drops in the shells—then a BOOM!—In the afternoon we had preliminary shooting on the machine gun. Your own gun doesnt have a recoil or doesnt scare you—but the blast of the gun on each side is bound to get you jumpy.—A cpl would be near you with field glasses to let you know where you'd hit. A certain cpl Yaverbaum kept screaming at me because when he'd tell me "bump one"—I'd press the trigger and rat-tat-tat . . three shots! . . Didnt know how to "bump one" until next day—

WEDNESDAY—Fired machine gun for record. Got all flustered but got 212—1st class rating (equiv to sharpshooter)—In the afternoon we fired anti-tank grenades from a special launcher on an Enfield rifle. We got quite a "kick" out of this—but being prewarned I had my gloves on my shoulder—Marching back I saw our camp looking like 1000 Fujiamas glistening in the sun. Suddenly what appeared like millions of ants boiled out of the tents. I'd swear the whole camp moved ten feet. We knew the answer—the PX truck had just arrived.

SATURDAY—The only thing I havent told you about is my M-1 lip. I had an M-1 thumb from the bolt—but my lip! Firing all day kept my thumb banging continually on my upper lip and cheek—didnt hurt much but drew many comments . . .

SUNDAY—JAN 2 have to brillo my mess kit—reclean my rifle—Chow has been OK—but have eaten much more stuff—cookies—cake—wonderful life—Bergeson eats nothing but bread—candy cake—cookies—walks thru line with closed mess kit (honest) Shot 180 yesterday—only expert rating in Platoon—. . . My feet are cold—G'bye—WRITE . . .

January 10, 1944

Heard the hikers almost doubletimed in—made the 18 miles in 4½ hours! Saw movie last night "A Woman of the Town"—OK—might see The Lodger tonight—I'll never forget the retreats we had. Here at camp we never see the buglar or flag—but there—what a sight—especially against the—sundown sky—I saw one magnificent sunrise too—all the tents shining and clean—I froze both ears! Theyre OK—Eating on the ground—crouched over—gobbling—washing in slop—shaving in the dark—one dipper of warm water in a helmet—another dream has passed—

A large number of long letters now come in bunches, reflecting the rapid and relentless succession of training exercises. Next: the dreaded Night Problem.

January 15, 1944 1100

Dear McTosh:

"They wont believe this at home"—the guy ahead of me said—and I smiled in spite of myself as I did many times last night—because I didnt even believe it myself! Here again is one of those "discretion letters"—daddy can read it if he wants to—but for gods sake, dont let the mater glimpse the bally thing—

Invariably it rains all day and all night when we are scheduled to pursue ourselves forth upon a night problem—This one was entirely tactical—For four hours we <u>could not</u> talk—sing—laugh—smoke or USE A LIGHT!!! This applied to cadremen and officers—too—We wore combat packs and gas masks—chin straps on helmets—NOTHING ON OUR PERSON COULD RATTLE—

As you can well imagine a rainy night is a dark night—Even before we are leaving the confinement of the 5th regiment, we can only make out a faint blob bobbing ahead of us—the pack of the man in front. As we are walking farther and farther it is getting darker and darker and rainier and rainier and pretty soon we can barely stay in line. All the while the silence is deafening. The only occasional noise is the grunts and groans produced when there is a sudden stop and the unknowing men behind pile up like an accordion receiving at the same time a bang in the jaw from a rifle butt—a poke in the eye from a bayonet handle, and a knock in the nose from a mess kit in the meat-can pouch—It goes on like this for miles—running—sudden stops—gurgled cries of the injured—

We proceeded thusly along Wood Road—hardly noticing the gallons of mud swirling about us—It was a practice bivouac march—at the end of which—in the blackness of the woods WE WERE SUPPOSED TO PITCH TENTS! Soon we start off a trail leading into the woods—now we had to hold on to each other. Every man felt like he was dragging the whole company along. I had on mom's scarf and nearly got <u>strangled</u> by the guy holding on to me—One poor Joe is tumbling down a hill on his snoot and soon, under the trampling of the oncoming hoard, is nothing more than a pile of miscellany. Naturally not seeing where we were—where we were stepping and not giving a xxxx we slipped on mud—stepped down heavily in unseen holes—tripped over logs—had branches snap in our faces—My poor M-1 got at least eight inches of mud driven up the bore from my falling and plunging it into the ground—However I am just gloating over the fact that my feet are still warm and dry when I hear Cpl Weedon—"God damn it—I wouldnt do this to a dawg." At once I hear splashing—and before I know it I am in the middle of a xxxx river! Now I was wetter than wet! Lt Tyler—known to assorted intimates as "Fearless Freddie" was forcing some guys thru the stream—I could hear screams of indignation and some of fear—Finally a character is grabbing Freddie and they both submerge—but I had not yet let go of the man ahead of me and was dashing crashing—splashing thru the jungle! To climax everything I hear a "Clang clang" meaning GAS so I let go of my man—grope for my gas mask flap—rip the thing open—and somehow get the thing on my head—now it is like being in a dark room with a bear—I can feel and hear his hot breath—only it is my own—so I stand there—hearing running—but I dont move—when I hear a sharp blast I take off the clumsy contraption—and try to get it back in the case—naturally I get all bawled up—so I just squeeze it together and proceed. I am utterly lost—but when someone runs by—I grab him and pretty soon I'm dragging a whole line again—Gad the confusion! By now we'd forgotten about tactics and shouted in muffled tones. I gather I am still amid the 1st platoon—I am very surprised to find myself in my own squad! We go off and were supposed to PITCH TENTS IN THE BLACK BLACK BLACK — We did not pitch tents! We just sat on some log someone stumbled over and cracked jokes! We sat around talking softly — not knowing what had been accomplished and not giving a xxxx

After everyone lost had been found we started back — worse than ever — getting strangled — Guys in the eighth co had lost rifles, etc but no lights could be used — so I guess they're just out $85 each — Many times we heard "SPLATS!" as personalities hit the ground — guy in front of me fell — I fell on top of him — guy falls on top of me etc etc — Much scraping as rifles hit helmets and heads — I SMILED JUST THINKING OF HOW I WOULD WRITE THIS TO YOU — I even closed my eyes — didnt make any difference anyway — mucho fun no?? Years later I hear sighs — open my eyes to find we are again on the highway (Wood Road) — A guy was groaning on the road — Seems his ying yangs had gone on a rampage — Lt Toop and Captain Herron were somewhere in the darkness — mad — disgusted — who wasnt?

AS SOON AS WE GOT OUT OF THE WOODS IT STOPPED RAINING — No trouble going back — seemed like twenty miles — all covered with mud — rifles in horrible condition — packs almost torn off — gas masks loose — flopping — SO WHAT HAD WE LEARNED

January 23, 1944

Sunday

LADDER TO ME FAMBLY
PART I

Dear Plitz:

Theeze surprise you — No? Well — our capitain is getting most happily and is allowing us to come in today to gat de shower and de shave. Than we leave for bivouac area again — Daddy wants to know how much weight I've gained — I weighed in at Fort Snelling at 127 — At Fort Snelling I gained 8 pounds — But after a month at Ft. Benning I still weighed 135 — Then — a month ago — BEFORE THE FIRST B. I weighed 141 — But I lost 10 pounds on the first B. Don't send me any more food — JUST LETTERS. I read your last one at least 30 times — in all types of Georgia jungle — at all breaks and in all positions — this should help to boost your ego — Here is the general situation — the whole thing is tactical — we <u>always</u> wear gas masks and steel

USO

MONDAY →

⑧ COMFORTER
2 BLANKETS
OVERCOAT

STEEL
HELMET
SHOES
ENTRENCHING TOOL

US

CANTEEN

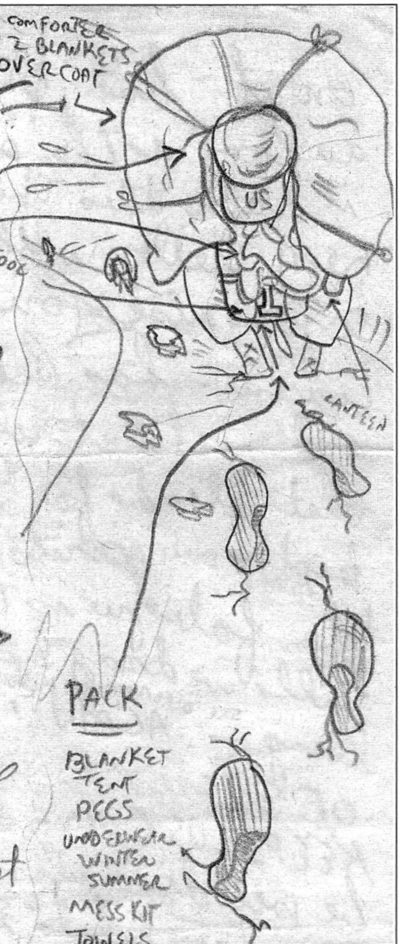

We left early in the morning looking like animated donuts - the man ahead of me -(and me) looked something like this ———→

How we ever got the thing together - even put them on will always be a mystery to me - my big horseshoe kept trying to fall off - but I kept it well forward on my neck - while walking along you feel as if you are falling backwords - my feet didn't

PACK

BLANKET
TENT
PEGS
UNDERWEAR
WINTER
SUMMER
MESS KIT
TOWELS
SOCKS
HANKIES
TOOTHPASTE, ETC
SHAVING STUFF

TOTAL WEIGHT:
105 LBS

(MISSING)?

helmets and have our rifle by our side 24 HOURS A DAY—MONDAY: We left early in the morning looking like animated doughnuts—while walking along you feel as if you are falling backwards—TUESDAY NIGHT & WEDNESDAY—January 25–26 We had an 8 hr—night problem—The first job was building a double apron barbed wire fence in pitch blackness— Another squad dug in—Our squad was on the left flank—the mission was to watch for the enemy (the major or the captain—who might find Lt Toop—the sgt—the cpls and <u>us</u> asleep—) I was part of a roving patrol who went around the listening posts at various time intervals—they were established to listen and watch for infiltrating enemy—Our password was shhh Little Lilliputions. All night long I kep hearing "Little"—"Little"—as the posts challenged the "enemy." ANOTHER 8 HR PROBLEM TONITE!

THURSDAY—My turn for KP again—(I worked 20 hrs altogether—they let us off at 2 in the morning and rolled us out again at 6—) Sorry—dont have time to finish this—but I'll write a long supplement later this week—

Ladder to Me Fambly
Part II

THURSDAY Got up in the usual confusion—I actually put on my leggings and fixed my blankets in my dark dark tent—In the morning we hippity hopped to our lecture area—and continued to fortify the positions we'd dug Tuesday. This time however, the squads switched areas—My squad took over the machine gun—I was the no. 1 man or gunner so I only had to carry the tripod—Thursday afternoon I was informed that it was my turn for K.P. so I quickly got together my blankets and comforter—and rode in on the mess trunk with the other KPS The guys gazed at me with envious eyes and begged me to go to the PX for them—I made no promises but agreed to do my best—Back at camp we went right to work—Me, Anders, Bregman and Greenrock had a beautiful location on top of the hill but a lt. came along and moved us—My slit trench was dug between two trees—I encountered a huge root every 1/2 inch I dug—all I had was a little shovel—I worked plenty late that night getting the thing dug—good thing it wasn't a fox hole—Trouble hadn't as yet started—In the morning—ye gods—groping around for my shoes—stockings—leggings—jacket etc— AND TRYING TO PUT THEM ON—Also in the cold on the ground?? When I appeared finally wearing (?) gas mask pack etc—I WAS ALL "FOULED" up—But in an hour the sun came up and we all felt okay again until:

TUESDAY: By now we'd been organized into a regular platoon —3 squads consisting of 2 scouts—squadleader—3 man BAR Team 4 Riflemen covering the flanks—an assistant anti tank grenadier—and the assistant squad leader & anti tank grenadier—in that order—I was a scout and alternated with the rifleman on the right flank—Besides this there was a squad as a machine gun section—The poor guys had to lug them around. Right then and there we learned the hideous nature of the surrounding territory. Tuesday morning we started "digging in" building a huge defense section—We all had definite jobs and definite missions—A tank trap was dug surrounded by mines—covered by 2 machine guns. And an anti tank grenadier—The squads were well dispersed—covering every enemy approach—My squad was in the rear: to support the forward units and protect the flanks and rear—We even had air guards—NO ENEMY WOULD PASS US! By the way—I had no shovel this time, so I had to dig my foxhole with my steel helmet—

In the afternoon (after 2 more hikes back & out) we had a problem: to get our men out of a difficult spot down a hill across a stream—thru a draw—and ATTACK AN ENEMY LODGED ON A HILL—Very much fun creeping up—and charging in upon the "amazed enemy" with bayonets— Wednesday afternoon we had the job of a suicide squad—raiding an enemy command post—blowing it up—and trying to escape alive to a secret rendezvous—

slong

Mort

WATCH for FURTHER ADVENTURES OF PRIVITCH ELEVATE

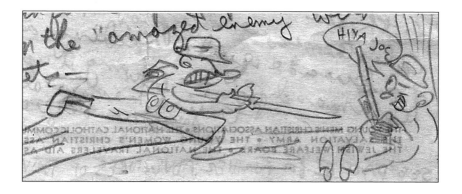

January 30, 1944

Dear Mom

I LIKED THIS BIVOUAC 50 TIMES AS WELL AS THE LAST—Unlike last B we had calisthenic and "group games"—we played "canteen ball"—the only trouble was the "field"—of course a few guys got konked on the head with the ball but—(not me) We had our shirts off—getting the full benefit of the intense sunshine—Another thing we did was just plain double time— we'd run round and round—until everyone was one big gasp—when about 100 had fallen out—theyd stop—I DID NOT FALL OUT—Thursday night was supposed to be the climax of everything—it was a company problem— involving everything we were supposed to have absorbed during the twelve weeks—they even issued us blank cartridges for ammunition—The whole thing was run by the trainees. We were made Lts., Sgts and Cpls—(I happened to be a Cpl) . . . Most guys tried to get killed so they could lie down and go to sleep—My squad was always in the reserve—didnt see much action and nobody got "killed"—I had a wonderful evening—we all sat around having a community sing—and general all-around good time— S'long for a while—bought you a wonderful book—"My Family Right or Wrong" by John Philip Sousa III. Burr—I missed "The Lodger"—It's in Atlanta now—

February 3, 1944

Szko:

One thing is sure—before or when we leave—our cadremen & officers go too—Toopy (Lt Harold V. Toop) has been assigned to Fort Leonard Wood, Mo., and leaves Friday—It was so sad this noon when we assembled and Toopy said goodbye to us and said he was proud of us. I'm such a sentimentalist. Tomorrow night we have a huge party.

It so happens you won't be getting a long letter again for quite a while—you see dear people I am changing my address. The next place you'll send letters to is a college—

February 1944

Hallo

I guess it's time to do a bit of serious talking—mom—old gal—as Burr tried to tell you—I think—there is no more ASTP—you see—the govt has not been getting it's quota of men—therefore the ASTP had to suffer—Right now I am permanently assigned to the 376th Inf—ASTP has been discontinued—already the colleges are losing all their 18 year olds—However there is such a thing as the ASTRP—In other words—17 year olds can be sent to school by the army—when they become 18—they are sent to Basic Training and from there are reassigned—such as I was—now I have told you this simply and frankly as I know you'd want me to—I know you wont be too shocked about it all—after all—it did involve 110,000 boys besides me—IF AT ANY TIME THE ASTP IS REORGANIZED—I will get a chance to go to school—since I have not relinquished my rights to it—But if this ever happens it will not be for a long, long time—so until then I'll go right on with my training—

We've put all ideas of school out of our minds—yet our education continues in many ways—not only do we acquire "Book larnin"—but we are learning how to live as men with men—and are all hoping that soon we'll be doing that in a peaceful world—I've said before—the Army is full of surprises—I just happened to get in the Army at the wrong time—but opportunity is always knocking—who knows what might happen tomorrow—

Yo honey chile

Mort

Early February 1944

Fort Benning

The man from the Red Cross really bawled me out yesterday—I was very surprised at your action—From now on I guess I'll have to write you all the time to keep you from bothering the Red Cross—I'm sorry that you worried needlessly too—You see I mailed you about 4 letters in the last week—

February 1944

Dear Veem

I'll forgive you for going to the Red Cross—As you see there was nothing to worry about—In Columbus F & E went to a corny show well equipped with about 25 crackly bags of candy—I got a good meal for 69 c—2 salads —2 bottles milk—string beans—French fries—big piece of cake—After the bus ride back Ellicott got a strange mania—he began picking up marked signs—and carrying them all over—even started to carry away some bleachers—Must have been the glorious harvest moon that did it— Tomorrow starts my 18th week at Benning—We know we're leaving starting Feb 20—but where???

February 17, 1944

Fort Benning

[postcard]
A miracle happened today! We turned in our rifles and bayonets—at least we wont have them to worry about when we creep and crawl—our shipping orders are in the orderly room—we'll go next week to Maine—Calif., Washington U at St Louis—Okla A & M—(???) I'd rather go to Calif. than Maine—so soon I'll be seeing Rudy Vallee's school [in Maine].
　　—We savagely G.I.d our hut this aft—prob'ly the last time we'll have this pleasure at Benning—

February 20, 1944

Columbus, Ga.

Hiya Mawm—

Since I'm in the beautiful Columbus USO—with a blonde on one knee and a Russian wolfhound on the other—having my shoes manicured and my hands polished—thought I'd drop you a bit of a note—Last night I slept over in Phenix City, Alabama. Fanset and Ellicott kept me up until 2400 drawing pictures with chalk. I've made myself some extra change around here—drawing cartoons on stationery and envelopes—Speaking of money —<u>please</u> let me know if you've received the money and stamps I've sent home—Each month I put at least $10 in one of your letters—and about two weeks ago I sent you $10.00 in war stamps—(The other fellows immediately cashed them in—but I hesitated to do it)—Besides this you should have received 4 or 5 $25 war bonds—To pep up a rather mediocre week—we went on a muddy 12 mile hike but it was in new territory—Most amazing—but without a rifle—I couldn't even feel the pack: (how different from 2 months ago—) Trudging along a highway I saw endless processions of funny-looking jeeps—Then I noticed a green Packard's bumper—On it was a red license with 2 gold stars on it. I looked in the back and sure enough I SAW MY FIRST HONEST TO GOSH GENERAL—(in person). Listen kitten—if there ever again comes a time when you don't hear from me (Thru no fault of my own) don't get exhistrocoloted (I made it up)—You know that after surviving all this basic training I certainly wont become an invalid overnight—You may not think so but I get time to think—things are sort of uncertain now as the result of ASTP being abolished—But the army is full of surprises and I'll try to take advantage of them—I don't know what is next on the schedule but I'll be patient—you too—Okay lay this letter aside—sing for me—I like to think of people singing

With "basic" completed, we successful trainees were assigned to the 376th Infantry Regiment of the 94th Division in Camp McCain, Mississippi. "The First Expert Infantry Regiment in the U.S. Army" cautions on its insignia "Don't Tread on Me." Since November 1943, it had been engaged in final precombat maneuvers, with emphasis on the squad as a fighting unit. In February, the regiment traveled to Holly Springs National Forest, Mississippi, for the first of intensive field problems, and thereafter moved quickly to integrate its new ASTP arrivals.

Camp McCain, Mississippi

March 2

Dear Mumu:

—I'd say conditions are 100% better than Benning's—although the training is tougher—a bit stricter but many advantages—a lot of older fellows in

my company—Don't worry about me—I'm way in the middle of
nowhere —all the sickness which usually invades the south is absent
here—the closest town is Grenada (5000)—no attraction. Memphis Tenn.
is 120 miles north. Oh yes my barrack is full of young fellows—many direct
from college—most of them never had infantry training—at least I'm not
in their shoes—Slong fer a while.

March 2, 1944

Toisday

[postcard]

More fun!!—Got another rifle today—A reject (as they all are) from
another battalion—What a mess—The black rings on the face of the bolt
must be an inch thick—Been scraping on 'em with steel wool for two
hours with little progress—Tomorrow we'll have inspection of packs &
rifles to find Sunday KPs—Oh well I have no money anyhow—Did I
mention that the farce examination found me 4 pounds heavier and 1 inch
shorter?? (maybe I did) NEXT WEEK WE BEGIN ADVANCED TRAINING WITH
A REGULAR COMBAT MANEUVER NEAR KING'S POND! One thing in our favor
is the fact that we'll come back here and sleep in the barracks at night
—we eat the noon meal on the field—This week we'll be divided into
battalions and regular rifle platoons—

March 3

Dear Possom:

BIG NEWS—Irony—Now that I'm out of the ASTP, I'm going to school!
WAIT A MINUTE—it aint what you think, Nevertheless I have been selected
as one of four men of my platoon to attend rifle grenade school—We'll
learn all about how to effectively knock out tanks, at comparatively long
ranges—The advantage of this new weapon is that it can fire from 75 to
200 yds and do damage—whereas a man can toss a grenade only 35 yds—

March 4, 1944

[postcard]

Much fun on KP (?)—whenever somebody wants something done—the
mess sergeant tells it to the staff sergeant. The staff sergeant tells it to the
T-3. The T-3 tells it to the sergeant—the sergeant tells it to the T-4. The T-4

tells it to the corporal. The corporal tells it to a cook. The cook tells it to one of his assistants. The assistant tells it to one of his helpers. The helper tells it to a KP pusher—A KP pusher tells it to a KP who tells it to the smallest K.P. *He* DOES IT—

March 1944

More excitement! I am now going to rocket launcher school—Last night we thought we'd freeze—but they brought us our overcoats in jeeps—much more consideration for the men than at Benning—How's my goldfish???

Got paid this morn—$43.30 (two months pay) We saw movies in the day room. I was sitting on a ping pong table—Capt Shetler was leaning on the edge—I got up to give him my seat—He is grabbing me by the pants and is pulling me back where I was—

March 16

[postcard]

I'm in what's known as a "line" outfit—more informality here among officers & men—our sgts—s/sgts—live right in the same barracks with us (unthinkable at Benning). Our plat. sgt is a Sgt Flynn—you ought to see some guys throw knives—here we have many discarded paratroopers who landed too hard on their heads instead of their feet. Shell shocked victims etc.—but the army has found that the infantry is its backbone—therefore all the best men (also us) are being put in the infantry.

March 19

Blackduck—

Getting to know the guys better—lots of cute Indian guys running round here—me like um—Fanset is next door now in a heavy weapons platoon—We really have characters here—one Tech Sgt from Brooklyn mumbles Brooklynese to our amuzement—He is telling us about "de an-op-heli-ez-mus-keeter"

March 25

Dear Flomz:

— Day le Grande —

(I) A new comet blazed across the Mississippi skyline on the morning of March 24, 1944. To be exact, it was good old Co A taking a nine mile stroll . . . It was the first time I ever got blisters on a march — 2 on my heels — and one on my little toe — (II) A couple hours later we (ASTP men) were hobbling up the same road — practically — we are arriving at the infiltration course — nobody goes thru it unless the grounds are sufficiently wet and muddy — As at Benning we started from a trench and crawled toward the machine guns — Pretty soon I hear a guy yelling "Lt. Cmere!" He is dragging out a man from the co who went before us — this G.I. had his hands across his face — he was crying — babbling — shaking — ye gods — what a thing to see before we go thru! I was glad when they lugged him out. The barbed wire was tough. Had to go thru on your back — Called "You'll be sorry" to Co B who stared at us — The hot sun quickly dried us into solid crackly dusty blocks — 40 little mudpies plopping down the road! (III) The schedule said we were to go thru I.C. again that nite! Guess what? — I got into the left side of the field this time — nice dry trench — NICE DRY GROUND!! the only thing that was bad were the tracers — It was impossible to see for awhile after they went over. Only time I got wet was when I squeezed into a truck next to some shivering lad — BUT WE WALKED BACK! Truck was for Co F — I cant understand it but I felt purdy good — air smelled good — after inhaling all the burned powder — Found out we had a full field inspection for the next morning — Had to scrape the gun clean — wipe it — brush it — oil it — Funny thing about the army — We'd loafed all week — then "pop" a day like that —

March 29, 1944

Camp McCain, Miss.

[postcard]

I'm living near a lake again!* We even thru stones in it this aft — For two days and nights it has rained — The big garden (to be) across from the Co. and the drill field are under 2–3 ft of water — Trees are sticking up from the

*The other lake is Lake Superior in northern Minnesota.

coffeeish liquid—The water is nearly level with the road—If it rains any more we'll be swimming to the rec hall—latrine and mess hall—Today we heard the "Articles of war"—required by army regulation—would have been a boring hour except T/Sgt McIntyre did pantomines behind unsuspecting Lt Stafford—and we nearly exploded—

Early April

Dear Gumf—

Oranges? Here I get oranges—apples—GRAPEFRUIT—pears—peaches— pineapple—grapes—cherries—everything but bananas—SEND ME A BANANA PACKED IN DRY ICE—Tuesday we leave for Holly Springs National Park 89 miles away—Tomorrow we drag a whole barrack bag full of our stuff out to the parade grounds—set up tents and display all our GI equipment—Theyll check to see if we have everything—and if it fits— Can you imagine seeing 5000 perfectly aligned tents and an equal number of sets of clothing all arranged alike? Besides that we'll stand by in ODs. I was supposed to be latrine orderly today but got out of it because of a little 25 mile jaunt I made last nite. I fired the bazooka yesterday!

APRIL 1944

Dregz

Last nite in the dayroom I was reading a book—asked Joe DeLibro what a few Italian words meant—He interprets them—pretty soon Bianchi is there—then DiPaula—then Nick Brocholian—Pretty soon every Italian in the co is swarming all over the book—pointing their index fingers— mumbling Italian . . . When I got the book back—it was too late to read—

April 6

Dear Uggo [brother]:

Yesterday we fired the bazooka. As group leader I had to pick my two best men—we fired with gas masks—steel helmets and leather gloves— (The rocket throws a lot of hot gas and particles behind it when it leaves the tube.) The firer hears a "whoopfh"—when he squeezes the trigger— but the loader is almost deafened—GI-BOUMPF! I missed the target on my first attempt. On the next shot I smashed it to bits so for my next tries— I had nothing but a pile of smashed wood to shoot at—

Near every range we fire on there's an old-time graveyard — saw one tomb of the "Hooper" family — Pa Hooper died in 1886 — 94 years old. On one little stone about a foot square was engraved — "Here lies Willie Gattle's foot — shotte off in aktion."

Once again the destination was Holly Springs National Forest, with the emphasis this time on combat maneuvers for the platoon.

April 10

Dear Gusim [brother] —

Trucks are bursting with men — rifles — steel helmets and packs — An attached trailer hauls our bulging rolls — The caravan of 12 trucks passed the Prisoner of War Camp — Aside from the tall wire fence that surrounds it, the place looks like a Miami Beach resort compared to McCain — Grenada was the first of three large towns we bisected. We were heading north toward Memphis. Now and then a female woman would appear and ejaculations would also. Those at the rear and front end had the best view of animate and inanimate objects — the majority of the occupants, bunched in the middle, would struggle madly when a landmark was announced. All during the 89 mile ride we saw more evidence of the real south — In Holly Springs however we saw many beautiful white mansions — I pitched my tent with Walter Bein. He has the reddest fullest lips I ever saw. His head is large and bony and covered with brown fuzz. In place of eyes he has hairpins which look like cracks in the glasses he wears — Nice kid. His family was chased all over Europe — out of Austria — (his birthplace) to NY

April 11 — Got up Fansetless. He'd left early with his platoon for their area. Each platoon was going on its own to run a 6 day problem! Trucks were to take us from our base camp — I saw how quickly it was being formed — dispensaries — kitchens — supply tents — motor pool — hqs — all camouflaged or under huge nets. sc* men were already stringing up wires, and jeeps were scurrying about delivering messages.

My platoon awaited transport on top of a high hill. Once on foot in this vast land, which made me feel Dan'l Boonish — we saw farm houses. Every once in a while we'd pass one buried in a clump of trees — They kept yapping dogs, hogs, and cows with longer hind legs than front (from climbing hills).

*Signal Corps

I missed the target on my first attempt
on the next shot I smashed it to bits
so for my next tries - I had nothing
but a pile of smashed wood to shoot at.
In the prone position I couldn't even see
the target — mucho fun — near
every range we fire on there's an old-
time graveyard (??) saw one tomb of
The "Hooper" family — pa Hooper
died in 1896 - 94 years old - on
one little stone about a foot square
was engraved — "Here lies Willie
Guttle's foot" - shottle off in
aktion"

Oh what a looong hot trek it was—By now I knew the mess was 1000 times worse than Lake Superior forest, 100 times worse than the Benning area—impenetrable treed areas—and bugs!—big beetles, little beetles, medium sized beetles, all colors, all kinds—flies, mosquitoes—What this forest called for was the Smithsonian, not us! We were enroute to a school house which we "attacked." We crossed millions of cotton fields and sloshed thru buzzing swamps.

April 12—We found our "enemy" playing craps in a field. They were happy to see us, because they had run out of change.

April 13—Right off the bat I get put on guard. This time I stand by an old oak and talk to myself and passing farmers. Then I get a job of latrine digger. So I dig a latrine. Then lie down—Ah! What a day—a nice little stream flowed at the foot of "my hill." I discovered a sleeper, "Farewell My Lovely" by Raymond Chandler—one of the cleverest, well written books I've read—I insist that you read it—

April 14—Every once in a while a sarcastic sarge behind me would help me along with a wrist breaking push. Near the crest of a hill he is becoming as cunning as a broken mouse trap. "When am I gonna get some milk—" he snippers—"This is tiring work." I catch on. I say "Sorry, Sarge, but there's a bull in my pack—no cow"—Suspicion crawls all over his face. "I do not think the bull is in the pack," he mumbles.

We'd seen striking examples of soil erosion, Mississippi featuring the phenomenon in king-size portions. The road is dropping off on both sides leaving us sky-lined on a narrow band of dirt macadam. Plagerizing a dime western—"One false step and we were goners!"—It was just like a fly on the edge of a bow tie as we pack mules tottered along.

I made the bivouac area—a thorn in nature's lap. First off the bat I get slapped on guard duty! I crawl behind an aged oak, disregard the sacred trust by sitting, and enviously eye the masses cooling their cooked countenances in a twinkling stream below me. Relieved, somewhat later, I rush up the hill, grab my stuff and Carl Floren and pitch tents. We just manage to get our stuff in when we hear the spatter of raindrops pounding the canvas. I frantically begin digging a drain ditch around the outside. Carl admires it. He says "Pretty nice ditch you dig." "Certainly." I get Barrymoreish. "Our family has been ditch diggers for generations. My family dug the ditch around King Arthur's castle—that's how I got my name—Moat-on Elevitch!"

April 15—Carl and I got guard duty—I finished enjoying "Farewell My Lovely" then read Agatha Christie's "The Patriotic Murders"—not so much action but extremely clever—Hot but a nice breeze—we were wonderful guards. That afternoon a dusty platoon glumly files by us—We learn that 100 yds away there had been a forest fire—destroyed 4 tents and made the area unusable—WE HAD NOT SEEN IT, WE HAD NOT SMELLED IT—WE'D HEARD NOTHING BUT THE SIGHING AND BUZZING OF OUR LITTLE KIBITZERS—

I pleaded with the sun to stay out but he was snotty as the devil and soon sagged out of sight. I smelled the earth and felt the silence and the darkness—up in the sky the moon shed its billowy cloak of clouds and warned me to get back inside—I did and had another session with Carl— Ventured a look again—Moon still glared at me but I felt peaceful and at ease. It said—go to sleep—I took its advice.

April 16—We had to make a nine-mile cross country tour—Oh what sights! Never have I seen such dilapidated, dissipated, worn-out, weather-beaten, decayed wrecks of houses—and they were inhabited—by people! The roofs were a tumbled mass of rotting shingles, the walls were scaly and cracked like chapped lips—The chimney if any was composed of broken bricks and mud had dried and the chimney had collapsed. We saw dozens of these mansions—always the staring eye of the well-fed farmer's kids and the hostile gaze of the mule munching on the front "lawn"—At last our route hit a dead end—or was it? Looming directly before us was a house! The Lt stopped and thought this one over—He checked his compass and his map—then we did it. OUR WHOLE PLATOON WALKED RIGHT THRU THE HOUSE!

Get set. Outside (wait a minute—I just want to assure you of the validity of this) back against a tree was the farmer—pulling on his corn cob—a hog was on the man's stomach! A frizzled purple woman held open the door for us—It had screening but resembled a lace doily on which someone had spilled acid. There were numerous flypaper rolls hanging from the ceiling—but the bugs only used the strips for a swing. A goose waddled into the hall and nearly got trampled. I expected to find hogs and cows in the kitchen but only found various examples of children—they managed to stare thru the grease on their faces and then backed shyly out of sight.

We talked about it for an hour—finally the Lt made a revelation—the farmer had given him a dozen eggs—

That small gesture (the eggs) was magnified when furloughs were granted, the last chance, everyone was certain, to visit home before overseas departure. It was a welcome rest, but I alarmed my father with my scarcely disguised apprehensions.

[May—undated]

Allo—

They gave me 13 days—of which about 5 should be spent in traveling— Dont expect to see much when you see me—I'm still pimply—my hair is halfway between long & short (<u>no</u> dandruff) my uniforms are not immaculate—Your son! I do not eat meat—either—The first thing I <u>do not</u> want to hear is "How do you like the army"—

May 17

Back at der Horror Haven of America!

It is so hot we are eating salt tablets and I am breaking into a sweat even while stroking an electric razor up and down my puss—From Duluth to Chicago was o.k.—Mom's sandvitches came in handy. Got into Chicago— purdy ride to the [Field] mooseum—got off in time to see an inspection of the Chicago police force—blue uniforms—black leggings and white gloves! Being very systematic I decided to pass down every corridor—starting at the right side of the top floor—I soon found out my mistake—I was wornout and hadnt seen anything good except the displays of child, frog and chicken birth which interested me . . I stood for a while on the front steps and looked at Chicago—It was sunny and cool out—I saluted a Chinese officer who bowed as he returned the salute—refreshing ride to Wrigly Field—what a stadium. THE SEAT HAD A BACK ON IT! I reclined there—my legs hanging over the seat ahead—and enjoyed m'self—See two old timers pitch—Curt Davis & Paul Derringer—Brooklyn takes a 5-1 lead—Cubs proceed to pound Davis and finally win in last of 9th 7-6! Got in Memphis at 0815—McCain—1230—Had only three sandwiches and coffee since Tues—noon—forgot to eat! Last night the Co had a 24 hr problem. WE HAVE ANOTHER ONE TOMORROW—I'm happy—console me

"AND DO TAKE GOOD CARE OF
YOURSELF — WON'T YOU?"

May 23

CAMP McCAIN

Just found out I'm on the 1st assault team operating a bazooka! Heard from "Yank" — got a big certificate signed by Sgt Marion Hargrove —

June 3 — It came to pass that it was a hot day during a class on map and area study by a sgt that couldn't speak — Many people got drowzy — Usually I sleep in these classes <u>but I wasn't this time</u> — A Sgt Turner had a brilliant idea to throw a guy sleeping in the drink — since I was the closest culprit I was selected — the river was only 3 ft deep — felt very refreshing on a hot day — I sat there and refused to come out — <u>No one hauled me out sputtering etc.</u> Finally Lt Stafford came down and told me to get out —

This incident was good publicity (unfavorable?) and put my name on the tongues of many — Even now I am referred to as "Sleeping Jesus." Ah fame!

Yank's Marching and Spam Club

Know All Enlisted Men by These Presents

that _____ Pvt. Mort Elevitch _____

is a member of YANK'S MARCHING AND SPAM CLUB and as such is authorized to sneer at Yank's editors whenever he feels that their judgment is poor. He is also authorized and urged to submit further gems of art and literature for so long as he shall remain an enlisted man and bear in mind that a stripeless soldier is the noblest work of nature. He is permitted to march with an added spring in his step, knowing that his future efforts will be judged by Yank's editors with a fraternal eye.

Sgt. Marion Hargrove
A Yank Editor

June 3, 1944

— EVENING —

The darkness was still far away when the fateful party entered PX 23 —
We strolled up to the refreshment counter, where we picked up four quarts
of beer and two milkshakes for me. Then goaded by the various members
of our party, I was escorted to the booth to join the others — with the
"handsome couple" — well advanced along the stages of intoxication.
Crogan's girl had dark hair and blue eyes — She had a cherubic face — she
was gorgeous, sweet, charming, adorable, and intelligent. After absorbing
most of the first "bot-tle" — Walt M Taylor was struck with the remarkable
whim of having me draw the fair lady's picture — I succumbed to their
wishes, futilely grasped a pen, and seated on a box, nose level with bottles,
I began to scratch. Co A was gradually assembling and recognizing us,
had gathered round to witness the spectacle: bottles peanuts and arms
constantly hovered in my view. Combine this with the moving head of the
sweet lady and you have a rather blurred image. Then the juke box spoke,
scattering its brutal blare. With this my admirers began using my recently
washed hair for a blotter. All this time the patient lady was bearing it, and I
was too. I had begun four times — Taylor was striving to lessen the horrors,
but would not move into the next room. The final blow came when Boomer
Flynn announced his presence with a lusty "YEEAHUH" I looked as if I were
recording an earthquake. The line of the lady's nose became as irregular as
a staircase. Mumbling something about being glad to've met her and being
sorry to've disgraced her, I rushed out into the cool night, but I could still
hear the rumpus —

June 1944

TELEPHONE CENTER
MEMPHIS, TENN.

Dear Zum:

We left on trucks early Wednesday morning and sat out 22 dust-clogged
miles — After riding 3 minutes we looked as if we'd been bathing in Face
Powder — or as if a spray gun had bombarded us with gallons of red brown
paint — Only our rifles worried us — they were "cast in bronze" — the area
we were in was the fortified area we'd attacked one week previous — It was

loaded with lurking duds—four men were walking along—one kicked a dud—KE-BLOWH! MEDICS! running! They put three tournaquets on his leg to stop the blood—leg later chopped off—the other three men were also injured. If the shell didnt kill 'em the jeep ride back to the hospital probly did. Got your letter with 3 dollars—I lost it all in a crap game with a pine tree—I dont need no money—LETTERS! The problem was cancelled cause 3 more guys got blown up—I slept in my rain coat at the side of the road—I was lying near an Indian name o' Fast Horse—Had quite a talk—When he went on furlough to his reservation in North Dakota they gave him a big feast & a tribal dance—(Sioux Indian)—One thing about these crazy problems—they always end

June 1944

Dear Fedle

Spend most of my time reading—On "The Affair of Hogsbottom" by Leslie Charteris—At the bazooka range the tubes had been going all day and were scorching hot—I hardly bothered to aim but got off my shots in a hurry before my ears cheek and shoulder got burned—

June

Gee filta wish?
[to mother]

Yesterday afternoon I was on a patrol with Sgt McLees and three others—we parked ourselves in a cool shady spot near a cool stream—here I devotedly watched the "boys" play in the sand—two of them were over 35—They made little battleships—PT boats, launched them, sank them with a barrage of sand—modelled the sand—fore-fingered roads—made "Sloppy Joe's Place" etc. Built Japan and demolished it on Dec. 7, 1944. Dont worry about the bazooka—It's just as safe as a rifle—Take it easy with temperamental Burr—Grad. [from high school] is a big thing

Late Spring 1944

Moomu

Undersecretary of War Patterson got here yesterday so we shot off a lot of ammunition and had a big divisional review for him—We can hardly restrain from laughing—when the poor battalion commanders scream out their inarticulate commands—

The regiment had achieved the Army's first Expert Infantry rating and received all due and colorful honors. Frisky from the attention, the battalions responded by demonstrating their firing power. Our entire division then motored to sufficiently rugged territory near Kilmichael, Mississippi, where we were thrown into realistic combat conditions, including the use of live ammunition and advancing under an artillery barrage.

June 19, 1944

RED BUG BLOOD
OR
MADMAN MALONEY'S MISSISSIPPI MOUNTAIN

Able one, Able three, over — able three, able one, over — Able one, able three, G-2 on P — Red Bug Blood — over — Even the rain didn't drown out the sputter of Boomer Flynn's walkie-talkie. Minutes later, Sgt Jim McLees, flushed but dusty, turned to us and gave us that Red Bug Blood password — thus starting the first night of the division's problem .. The ride out was a longie — nearly 30 miles — past Winona and Carmichael. Near this latter town rain clouds bunched up and belched. Soon icy streams sliced down our backs and began soaking into our shoes. The only bit of reading matter I'd brought along, a Time, was a pulpy mess splattered to my pack — I had a plug in my rifle but the rust was pushing it out. On the side of a road we were informed Co A was to pull outpost. My squad formed a half-moon in the woods guarding the artillary gun. We had three sentinels — one to be "awake" at all times. We wrapped up in our dripping raincoats, used our unopened rolls for pillows and promptly kissed the ground.

After sleeping under forementioned conditions, there we were — the usual, sloppy, crumpled dazed things that appear during these problems — I was awakened by Francisco gabbing with Lt. Dunville who was satisfied he had a "good, wide-awake crew."

We were but 50 feet from the gun, easy range of a clever enemy, so we had to move. Shortly harnassed up, tramped into the sunlit vines and loaded on a truck which bumped us into the wilderness and left us blinking at Mississippi 82. Now we were guarding a road block near the highway — I was part of a bazooka team. A dip in the highway revealed anything which passed, yet screened us (me and Fast Horse) from view. Gorgeous gals from nearby Winona began scouting for their husbands. A car stopped and two young ladies wearing some perfume (not much more) daintily tripped in front of our noses and popping eyes—Fast Horse was shaking in the bushes, bringing prickly things down on my head—Soon we heard the familiar boom of T-Sgt Flynn and the bow-legged one appeared—closely followed by Jim McLees. Flynn just sat there under a tree—in plain view of the road: "I could go for dat little one."

All we did then was sleep, eat . . I managed to pry apart some of my Time and read it word for word—After a while most of the fellows were standing right in the road—The great day had only started . . Near eventide we began to pay for the ease of Monday & Tuesday—with rolls and all we staggered up the dirt road—For some reason the gas mask & cartridge belt just don't jibe—The mask keeps pushing down on the belt, and the belt keeps pushing down on your hips—The arm cannot feel free since it must hang outwards to allow for the gas mask . . My roll, naturally, was banging against my stomach—and my shovel was banging against my rear extremities providing quite a bang-up time. Then we gave up—after consent by Lt D we fell over and just lay by the roadside mute and unconcerned. Two trucks came by 2100—we were to push off to our jumping off spot 11 miles away—The "enemy" had been reported dug in in the vacinity of Able Hill—

The first five miles we must have done in 45 minutes—WITH ALL THE SUDDEN CRASHING STOPS—(remember the descriptions of night marches?) This time we had vehicles with us—blackout driving. The banshee cry went up—we had a rest while an ambulance crept up to load in the remains of a T-Sgt a jeep had run over—Later on an ASTP boy from Florida was mashed to death instantly by a truck (so I was told). We went 6 solid hours and covered but 20 miles—Hardened infantry men with 18 mos. behind 'em babbled that it was the worst experience they'd ever had—Example of why we love our leaders: S-Sgt Sullivan—a spark-plug veteran of pre–Pearl Harbor days—kept running up and down the column keeping tab on stragglers bleary-eyed and beaten—I don't see how he kept up the impossible task as long as he did. *Private* Sullivan is being transferred soon.

Dropped exhausted in a field covered with dead lumber—my fatal mistake—the chiggers had a feast that night. They gave us no water that morning—HAD NO WATER FOR 16 STRAIGHT HOURS—We just sat around and never moved when they told us to dig in—as expected they halted the digging and pushed us off again—I don't know how I did it but I got half a mile away to a well—and got cold water. I returned and slept except when I had a medic put ointment on my chigger bites and fix up my blisters. My socks were like old chamois skin, my feet like dried prunes.

We got up to go and <u>I missed my rifle</u>—I knew where I'd left it—at the well —I'd forgotten it and hadn't even missed it all this time. Naturally that M-1 wasn't there when Sgt Jimmy and I panted up—Our Co had shoved off. A farm boy said a Lt had picked it up in a jeep, meaning the farmer probly had it in the house—we didn't argue—I was in for an $82 bill and plenty of punishment (DON'T GET EXCITED—EVERYTHING COMES OUT OKAY).

Finally reached the Co in the new area—Chased around till sundown inquiring in every co in the battalion—but was rifleless when I collapsed in our biv area—"Pray to God," the 1st Sgt told me . .

Had supper, fresh water, pushed off into enemy territory—Able Hill was close by—Next morning there'd still been no attack—our clever foe had given us the slip and had pulled stakes for "Charley Hill" BEHIND us— We moved closer to the hill and waited—we would have to attack over high sticky grass, vines, logs, mud and swamps, all crawling with chiggers, snakes and lizards. Lt Hodges had popped off to an umpire and was to be court-marshalled. Lt Dunville was so tired he hadn't bothered to inspect our positions and hadn't ordered us to dig in—Sgt McLees, Bryson, Springsteen, Brown, Tipton and me were all jabbering together, shirts off, not dispersed—An umpire strolls up. What a character—in the army for 9 years and never been home! Another umpire surveys us: "Freeze your dogs—Don't you know you're to keep your shirts on? Who's your squad leader where's he at anyone dug slit trenches?" He was worse than the sun. Kept jotting down in his little black book.

The attack began after chow. What a barrage! Shell after shell after shell—After dark it was beautiful—spectacular and noisy—white phosphrous shells blazed in the distance—smoke formed crazy billowy patterns and absorbed thousands of brilliantly colored stars from parachute flares—Tracer bullets whined and tore and disappeared and came again—It never stopped for four solid hours—right overhead the cak cak cak of the machine gun kept me awake—Up at 0430 to eat chow, but there was no chow—So with no breakfast, no water, no hope, we began our attack . .

Cool under an enormous beach umbrella Genl Maloney and his staff watched us from a lofty spot atop Able Hill—we could see them—tiny dots—They'd undoubtedly had a shave, bath, hot meal, and were driven up there in a command car to watch us . . Certainly it's not like this overseas— Genl Clark, Bradley, Patton, Alexander, Montgomery are with their men—

So we began our final drive—thru that mass of Mississippi stubble— creeping closer to Charley Hill—I didn't even think about my rifle—gave my clips of live ammunition to others — dragged along not knowing the situation or our orders — We were in an area loaded with duds but no one seemed concerned — they were offering fortunes for drinks of water — And then you wait and wait — you sit in the sun and wait — and do nothing. The men are keyed up, they want to fire, but there is no order — so someone gets up, points his M-1 in the air and pulls off 8 quickies — You can feel the surge of relief when the order to fire and advance is given — The men shoot off everything that's stored up inside them — You can hardly see them in the smoke but you can hear 'em shout — Every once in a while we'd turn around and look back at Genl Maloney — puffing his cigar under the umbrella on good old Able — How the men cursed thru their beards! The faces were studies: hot, plastered with filth, quivering — The eyes I'll never forget — Then the cam that broke the strawls back: The 302nd was coming up behind us — and not realizing it — they started <u>firing live ammunition at our</u> backs: Five tense moments before it was stopped.

By now we were in such a state of confusion that Maloney split his gut and called the whole thing off. It was 1530 Friday. Trucks pulled us in — we had a bite to eat — but most of the fellows swarmed the PX, relieving it of everything eatable. There'd been 600 casualties on this problem — 400 in the hospital from chigger bites —

A guy in D Co had my rifle. Got it Saturday morning — I keep asking myself — "What did I learn?"

With the Normandy invasion well under way, preparations for embarkation were accelerated.

June 1944

TELEPHONE CENTER
MEMPHIS, TENN.

Dear . . . . . [brother]

Big changes are coming about for you — and me too methinks — Our sailing tickets are ready — All new equipment is arriving — They say that we have 30,000 prs. of white leggings, gloves and belts to wear upon occupying a town —

Naturally — nothing is definite — although check ups on service records and clothes are being made — This news is for you only — unnerstand? —

A big three day problem tomorrow is commencing — we carry full fields in trucks — Big emphasis now on gas protection — First aid — ahem —

Hope I'll be in shape for another week-end—
Going to "Eve of St. Mark"—
Every co. has pets in the barrack—we have dogs—squirrel and a snake
—Saw one guy with a baby fox on his shoulder
The bugs are bad—Flies especially—Out in the woods—red pin heads
—known as chiggers—bite themselves into your skin and produce blotches
and the misery of itching—
Our radios played today—speculations and arguments were heavy on
the outcome of the invasion—but over confidence was absent. We just go
on with our schedule—waiting for the day we'll be running up the
beaches—
The heat and dust aint getting me down—just makes me see the futility
of all this and more. You are the only one near my age connecting me with
a human bein's life—That is why I must have your letters. Constantly my
thoughts and thoughts of the others dwell on their high school days—the
last of civilian life they knew—now you can keep "me" going with your
experiences—
As I have said—the army has given me some things I've never had or
done before—but it has made my faults stand out—I hope I'll get a chance
to get over them—but in case I don't I want to be satisfied that you are
doing the things you want to do without being in constant turmoil—Sadly
enough—this is all very silly—which shows you what happens to some
people in the army—

July 6, 1944

CAMP McCAIN, MISS.

[postcard]

At last zumtink heppent—a nice Lt was joking with me—wanted me to lie
down by some grenade cases he thought were full—Then he goes down
into a dugout by the firing line. Blam. 1st one goes off—Blam—No. 2—
We hear Lt Decker (in charge) yell "Medics"—Find this other Lt slumped
out—gasping—blood pouring out of a big hole in his right chest—Particles
in a 1000-1 chance—had come almost 100 yds—thru trees—over a big
sand mound—and had pierced this guys pulmonary artery—collapsed his
lung and killed him—Quite shocking—so fast—so near—called off the
firing for the rest of the day—start tomorrow at 0700—No matter how
many precautions are taken someone is bound to get it—always the good
and valuable—

July 8, 1944

[to Burr]

When I send my next pkge I'll include a pocket book—Two stories in particular are examples of ones I've been reading—melancholy—people on verge of insanity or death—one by Conrad Aiken is strange but a masterpiece—"Sweet Snow, Silent Snow"—I'll also send a piece of the grenade that killed the looey—I can understand your feeling of impatience —of wanting to run—So far you've had more freedom—although you may not think so—than service life will give you—I never have advised you on anything yet—This wanting to get away can be satisfied—at school in several months—I may send you money one of these days—and a ticket to join me somewhere. IF YOU SEE A GOOD THING IN THE NAVY NOW GRAB IT—but I can see you hesitating right now—A year from now there'll be that much less dirty work to do—I'll be in the thick of it—I assure you— there is no sense in destroying the remarkable Elevitch clan completely —Maybe I better get on my rifle—I hear Boomer coming

A soldier accepted a New York USO attraction—an address of a blind date—He finally found the lady's apartment building, walked upstairs, found Apt E and rang the bell. Soon a lovely vision appeared before his eyes, the most gorgeous girl he'd ever seen—he was drooling with anticipation—"Come inside," she rippled melodiously, "I think I hear someone coming." Once inside the dim interior of her room, she pressed herself against him—her lips were cool and soft—"Tell me," she whispered slyly, "What's the most sensitive part of my body?" "Your ears"—he whispered back—She was bewildered—"My ears?" "Yes," he answered —"A while ago you said you heard someone coming—it was me!"

Hlo—Just finished eating a super-deluxe pedigreed seedless orange .. FOR THE FIRST TIME IN THE ARMY—I HAD A CHANCE TO DRILL A PLATOON —only three of us had nerve enough to do it—more than just hut-hut-hut-too-thre-foh"—now I see why sergeants have such dry throats and long for beer—

[undated]

You asked about my leetle pals—JOHN W. FANSET: Eighteen years old— pimples on face—dark brown eyes—light hair—lived in Watertown, South Dakota—His dad is dead. Has a brother overseas in Italy—Eats tons of candy and ice cream without ill affect—Has a light voice—but a very unusual laugh sounding like a Ford motor in a Koala bear—Acts sorta like

July 23, 1944

THE AMERICAN DOUGHBOY*

Here is the American Infantry Soldier——the
Eager, deadly master of victory — their
Nicknames: Valor, Staunchness, Heroism.
With chin held high, the flush of confidence
Mirrored in shining eyes, these three men
Represent the spirit of the freedom
To come; and the unrelenting courage
Of future America - - - - -

★ THRU COURTESY OF PVTS. SIDNEY ELLICOTT, JOHN FANSET, AND MORTON ELEVITCH 49ᵗʰ DIV.

a kid—Has to be dragged out of bed in the morning—Can be serious minded—DOESN'T DANCE—Inclined to be bashful with girls—Easy going —likable.

SIDNEY RONALD ELLICOTT: Eighteen years old—blazing blue eyes— light hair & complexion—lived in Denver, Colorado—moved to Oakland, California—Attended Oakland Tech High—Has a sister—writes to many girls—Eats tons of candy & ice cream without affect—loves potato chips— Has a rather crackly voice with a slight western accent—nervous—directly opposite character of Fanset—except for silliness—is sharp—sarcastic— never seen him dance—Will drink and smoke—

Both of 'em are smart—Fanset especially—I can influence both—like Burr does to N. & J.—Well, do you approve of my friends?

Camp Shanks, in Rockland County northwest of New York City, was constructed as the world's largest staging area, the port of embarkation for more than 1.2 million men and women on their way to North Africa and Europe. It also accommodated wounded, returnees, and POWs. After lectures, equipment checks, and abandon-ship drills, we all abandoned the camp as well, with brief recreational passes to surrounding towns and New York City.

July 30, 1944

July toitieth

EASTERN NORTH AMERICA
[Camp Shanks, New York—prior to departure]

Madre:

Now that I'm sitting down writing this, the whistle'll prob'ly blow, but I'll do as much as I can. I'm on the front porch of our barracks, facing main street, where trucks and people are going by. A volley ball game is in noisy progress to the right.

You inquired about coming to New York to see me. I can tell you right now that both of us would be disappointed—since I dont know if I'll ever get there or when.

Last night I was lucky enough to get free before the last show started. However, the sky was reddish when I left—and by the time I'd reached a library a squall was screaming toward me. Got inside before water & hail stones descended. Couldn't find much—but I got another James Thurber masterpiece — "My Life and Hard Times" — It is identical in style and subject to "My Family Right or Wrong" — but is instead a collection of short stories —

The sky cleared, and I plunged into the crowd, bubbling in front of the theater — In we went — I wandered down the aisle, moved into a likely seat and beheld gazing at me with pale blue eyes — none other than Sidney Ellicott!! We watched with conflicting emotions — a most unusual picture — which will undoubtedly be discussed by widowers, old maids or mozambique gorillas who happen to see it. It keeps building up — thru the means of a wonderful musical background — and the acting of Bette Davis — until it reaches a climax — as "Bigeyes" gets made (by the make-up artists) a hideous plastery face — That, I liked — especially when she got diptheria — Be sure and see it — Name: "Mr. Skeffington" — (Claude Raines) — Afterward we talked — and I headed homeward.

Just learned that I am authorized to speak of at least one state we saw on our trip — I might as well take advantage of this — since I've mentioned nothing so far.

Probably the prettiest state I've seen since I've left home is Virginia. The farther we went, the more I enjoyed the scenery — Blue ghosts of mountains rising far in the horizon — silver streaks shimmering where the sun creased the crevices. Huge masses of hills — covered with a solid, soft carpet of green. Valleys and rivers — Little towns with quaint names like "Sweet Briar," reposing amid the magnificence of nature. Many of the homes and buildings were equal in beauty to the scenery — always set off by expertly trimmed shrubbery — impressive in many shapes and colors.

It seemed that everything was green — even the water, which we saw in rivers and streams. Speaking of water I was interested to see the process of aeration — where water is purifyed by spraying it upward — Outside of [deleted by censor] we saw blocks and blocks with a silky cover of spray — glinting as it wavered in the sunlight.

Sgt Flynn had a pair of binoculars, which we found extremely useful — So did Oliver, our porter — and two of his colored friends, who used them with sly excitement to spy upon lovely colored ladies — of which there were many.

The last thing I remember about Virginia is a mansion — dark and imposing — framed in the greenness — Small against the tall white columns in front — was a girl who waved to us. Naturally the train shook with our reply — but her lips remained tight — she did not smile — . .

August 2, 1944

Hello Oscar—I saw New York last night—

I

The ferry took us from New Jersey to 42nd St., Manhattan, bringing the skyline closer and closer in a misty panorama. The ferry was wide and sturdy, and puffed along at a fair rate of speed, swooshing up the Hudson River. We were packed together at the rail, cooling off in a stiff breeze. . . . The ferry was lavishly decorated—styled in fashions of early twentieth century and flashed the name of "Stony Point." We saw the bustling of the biggest port in the world. Far off to the right—the Statue of Liberty maintained its tolerance of the seething city it guarded. The ferry grunted up to the dock and sqooshed to a stop.

II

Forty-second street looked bare until the soldiers hit it. Fanset, Kettler and I were at high speed, running a daring race in order to assure ourselves of entertainment later. The buildings still looked far away. An old woman shuffled past us clutching a basket. She had her eyes tightly closed, and was shining like a lonesome coyote. An old horse with large black eye shields sneezed and rippled off flies—while his greasy-dark master attempted to get rid of rotting oranges in a decrepit wagon hanging from the animal's scrawny shanks. Three Italians glared at each other and bit off screams with their decaying teeth. One, a hairy woman, withdrew a paw from beneath a roll of her grimy clothing and struck her daughter in the face. Taxis shot around like yellow greyhounds yipping their horns. Half a mile later—a sweaty mile—Times Square loomed to our left—We were on Broadway. The scene was not startling—it was too familiar—Only the signs jolted us. They were too large—much too large. No-one could miss seeing them. They all advertised movies. Around the Times building the constant flow of latest news ran and quivered and blinked its timely message. We went on—in Indian fashion—Fanset running interference. At Madison we saw a service center—Yes—they had plenty of tickets to Oklahoma!—for August 9.

On under the mammoth buildings—Empire State bulking high and mighty to the right. At 99 Park we again verified my theory—You can get more by yourself—than by letting Service Centers try to help you—Only got a ticket to "Famous Jury Trials"—Told us we might possibly get tickets to "Ten Little Indians"—Pick Up Girl—Left in a huff—speeded back to 42nd—caught a st. car to Times Square.

III

The tickets for "Ten Little Indians" cost me $2.40 each—They were for the balcony. The Broadhurst theater was on W. 44th in the midst of dozens of others—Across the street was "Oklahoma" and "Follow the Girls"—We could have seen "Follow the Girls"—Standing up—But the Donk that Strawed the Brokeys Back was to come two hours later when we learned we could have seen "One Touch of Venus"—such is life. It was 7:45 pm as we entered Stage Door Canteen, clomped down a vividly decorated winding stairway, received a ticket from a pair of teeth and entered the fabulous room of stars. The show was in progress. We picked up milk and a sandwich at the bar and watched a blue clad 4-F sweat. He was the best dancer I've seen. A girl asked me about my Infantry badge, whose blue was the color of her eyes. We left after gazing at the hundreds of original drawings on the wall—The smoke followed us out into a drizzle outside. But we were warm.

IV

Broadway—Times Square—the people—"Do you have trouble with your hair"—the man looked like a hypnotist with fallen arches—whatever that is—He used guinea pigs to demonstrate his hair-restorer. We raised our hats and revealed our fresh g-i's—past the automat—Rockefeller center welcomes us.—The Music Hall had a lobby—all reddish and plush and lavish—Radio City!—Up and up 1400 feet a minute—out onto the roof 70 stories high—usually I get very sentimental—you know—I just looked at it. The most magnificent thing I will ever see—New York at night—But I just looked at it. It was cool up there—thru a telescope we looked thru skylights and windows into offices and homes. Most amazing. Signed my name in a book with those of hundreds of Duluthians. The last longing look—You feel so humble—An NBC studio on the sixth floor—breathtaking beyond words—seats that fit themselves to your habits—The program was "Let Yourself Go"—sponsored by Eversharp Pens—Milton Berle, Roy Block and His Orchestra—I can't explain it—but a minute after youre there Berle has you laughing—not too much at his words—his actions—He kisses men with bald heads—"Stick your finger in his ear and use him for a bowling ball"—He spits water all over—He insults late comers—The program starts—the smoothness is unbelievable—I am in ecstacy—Berle wears a brown hat—The jokes are good but they aren't needed to bring laughter—It all runs off like a dream—commercials— band numbers—singers—stooges—imitators—blended in and carryed along in such a way that made this my favorite experience.

V

Times Square—Buy you present—ice cream—subway station—hotel lobbys—

VI

The ferry went back across the river—

August 6–12, 1944

Our ferry now became the gigantic and speedy liner Queen Elizabeth, twelve thousand of us swamping her decks. We joined a convoy, zigzagging to avoid the enemy, taking us to Greenoch, Scotland . . .

SPRAY

I

The caravan moved slowly, plodding along in unbearable heat, pausing only when the endless procession became jammed with wild disorder. The camels were giving valuable experience to their unusual stomachs, for they'd been without water for hours. True, their canteens were full, but the head sheik had clabbed his stubby hands and ordered that no water be taken.

The stay at the last oasis had been extremely pleasant, but it had lasted far too short a time. There, the tribesmen—even their beasts of burden— had been royally entertained. They had feasted like kings, slept like kings, and read like kings. There was, in addition, a memorable visit to a flourishing community—the largest village in all the land, bursting with gayety, richness, and an abundance of abstract abandonment.

The camels thought of this, even though their masters pushed them on, forcing them to tremble with fatigue. Accustomed as they were to toiling with the weighty wares of warriors, a full field pack, roll, overcoat, steel helmet, gas mask, rifle, and dragging duffle bag presented a major problem.

Moments before, they'd been cooled by breezes from a cold, blue stream, whose waters were churned beneath them by their craft, a large canoe stretched tight and firm by many hides.

The animals' dark docile eyes soon grew round with wonderment as they viewed with awe a gigantic Arc—far greater than Noah's, on which their forebears had tread so long ago.

Once aboard, they struggled through tangled mazes of hallways, and at last were settled in their cramped stifling quarters, where they sweated amid stacks of equipment, which strangled the small amount of light available. Each animal was provided with a stretched canvas suspended on a frame. Once in their resting places, they eventually began to twist and turn, and a terrific din, fierce as the cracking of a thousand muskets, filled the choking air.

The corridors became filled with many who sought a slight refreshing draft. They were very, very tired but from only a few could be heard the soft, secluded sound of soothing sleep. . . .

II

Somehow the story didn't turn out that way. Two hours after we boarded the vessel, we stripped off our soaked clothing and pulled on fatigues. This meant but one thing—further labor.

We were herded down a flight, through a broad, indirectly-lighted, brown and burnished bronze foyer, into an incredible mess hall. It was far different from the others I'd seen. The table tops were green, and along the edges were strips of silver metal, instead of gum. The ceiling was high—decorated with stars concealing tiny sprinkling systems. Soft light, elaborate trimmings, and mirrors produced a startling effect, giving one the feeling of being in the dining room of a large hotel.

But we weren't on a sight-seeing tour. A captain began to spout to our two assembled companies, complimenting us and honoring us. We were to be allowed to feed our fellows—every day—all the way across!

Understand now—the work was not hard—it was the time element that mattered. Of course, we did get four hours off each day. Then too, we didn't have the worst job. We were merely table waiters, who received various colored tickets from certain individuals, and proceeded to dash to the immense, immaculate kitchen with aluminum-ware pans in order to secure food.

However, it wasn't as simple as all this. Men coming in the mess hall, men going out of the mess hall,—table waiters going into the kitchen, table waiters coming out of the kitchen continually became involved in sort of a wild merry-go-round, causing us to scream with rage, bang into each other, drop slop, and slip on same.

Upon arrival at our pleasant working place, we rubbed our bleary eyes, threw benches off tables they were stiffly reclining on, and provided a terrific clatter and clanging of pans and trays, which skidded on the table top and crashed to the floor.

One man (we worked in pairs at each table) grabbed for a deep round pan, swished down an aisle, and butted into a boiling bread line. The other man swept a biggish coffee pot into his grasp and bustled off for the muddy java.

Back again at home base, they would begin to scream loudly joining the growing chorus of "TICKETS!" Clutching a blue square, I'd whisk a longish pan to a counter, shoving and pushing until I had completed a cycle and had received my meat, vegetables, or whatever the menu might offer. In the meantime my partner would handle a handful of tickets, and bring back jam, butter, cheese, cold meat, salad and fruit.

We'd slide around a corner, shoot into the mess hall, collide with six or eight others, scrape our food off the ceiling, remove our head from somebody's mouth, and continue the mad race, arriving at our table to see twenty-eight hands materialize to sweep every morsel of food from us.

Staring at our empty mess kits, my cohort (a Cpl. Dye) and I often wondered if we'd get something to eat at the next serving. We learned to inhale food en route, although one hand carrying was difficult. If we ever collided with a chunk of cheese in our mouth, orange coils would shoot out from between our teeth, looking like a bunch of Squibb toothpaste tubes being squeezed simultaneously.

As the days passed we found short cuts in our game, and became more and more skillful at eluding other food bearers and crowds. We hoarded tickets, which enabled us to have the table set before the main bulk appeared. At that time we'd be gone, either to the deck for a breather, or out in the foyer for a half hour of reading or resting. Usually in the afternoon we had ample time to shave or even take a bath. One great trick was to have a man at the head of the wash line before the final meal was served. What a scrambling and gnashing of teeth there was then! With our pans washed, we again rubbed clean the table top, put up the benches, and took off.

The best working agreement was finally settled on sometime later. We began working in two hour shifts—without that I assume this masterpiece would have never been completed. We found out that one man could capably fill the job and cut down on the number and confusion of the waiters. At the same time this luckless individual bore the brunt of the troubles. Usually the first drooler at the table would gobble up half the chow before the others were seated. On most items, seconds were impossible to get.

There were some Britishers working in the kitchen. They reminded us to "mind ourselves" as they swept by with covered heaping trays for the officers, who received a more appetizing meal than we did—as could be expected. I unintentionally insulted one Englishman dealing out bread. Sniffing a delightful aroma of cinnamon buns, I inquired—"What's that I smell?" "It's not me, I hope," he coughed in typical British humor. "No," I returned innocently—I assure you—"I mean that good smell."

All in all we got on famously with them and they provided us with much diversion. They seemed to know more about our democracy than many of us did, and could out-talk the fellows on many subjects.

These "Limeys" (as we called them) had definite accents, which we attempted to copy, and did poorly, irritating them "no end." I don't blame them for disliking Americans who "chuck their weight about."

Working like this together leads to better understanding in the long run —as we found out.

We also had a few advantages in being allowed almost a complete run of the ship, whereas other groups wearing red, white, or blue tags were restricted to their areas. The table waiters wore large round white buttons with a blue eight on them. We were supposed to have special movies, but I never saw one.

Fanset and I eventually roamed the whole ship, exploring every corner. Someday I'll tell you about it.

Our task allowed for great groaning on our part, and a groping about for sympathy, but everyone did have to admit that we got more to eat then the other enlisted men. Eating two meals a day, we got a good share of potatoes and meat, no sweets—except canned fruit. We had oranges twice and apples once. When eggs were served they had to be hard boiled, since they were handled so rough.

We worked on hot and cold days. We really sweated even without jackets. Our bare arms and backs became streaked with jam and gravy spots, resulting from the fray. The front of our pants resembled a pig's snout which had just emerged from a garbage can.

The food <u>wasn't</u> exactly as we'd been accustomed to, mainly because it was all steamed, <u>but</u> I reiterate: eights ate.

III

"The moon was bright, and late one night in Eric's humble home, the madman tossed upon his bed, and scratched his sweating dome"—

Funny how you think of things like that—I'd written it years ago.

It was our first night on the ship. Fanset and I were far away in a quiet cabin, hanging our heads out the port-hole. We watched the buildings in the distance fade and then suddenly stand out in the dusk. We watched the little lights pop on and spread and grow like friendly beacons. We saw the water far below, glossy ripples spreading as tugs and barges chugged and blew their smoke out of their hair. Things like this make people talk. Maybe the talk doesn't make sense, but they talk anyway.

IV

The ocean was a different color every morning. Every picture that's been painted of it no matter how extreme, is correct. Shades of blue, as varied in depth as the article in a pawn shop window, shifted and eddyed and changed into browns, and greens, and purples, and greys. The sun kept a constant rainbow shimmering in the spray gushing from our bow.

It's a thrilling experience to hit the deck, creep forward, sniff the air, watch the foam and white caps, and squint ahead and around at the water. The wind, occasionally, became strong and chilly. It would literally blow you about and scream and laugh in your face. The water was usually calm. We could see it rise and fall—though below, the ship <u>would</u> totter but it caused no trouble in the mess hall (there was enough already) and only a few became really sea sick. The ocean is wonderful to stare at for hours at a time. You never tire of it—it never tires of you.

V

They didn't know on which side of the ship it could be seen from, so I made a hasty decision and crowded over to an open window. It was green on top and red-brown on the bottom. The sun got in my eyes and made me squint. The ship was moving fast, and not many noticed the Statue of Liberty. . . .

VI

We didn't just work and sleep and eat. Although there was a library with good books, I never patronized it as I had all I wanted. I <u>did</u> get there—the one page paper I've enclosed—"Ocean News."

Books I read were Thurber's "Middle-Aged Man On a Flying Trapeze," Thorne Smith's "The Bishop's Jaegers," Emily Kimbrough's "We Followed Our Hearts to Hollywood," Louie Bromfield's "Mrs. Parkington," Howy Spring's "My Son, My Son!" and "Mr. and Mrs. Cugat" by Isabel somebody.

Movies were shown up on deck at nite but I never got near them, nor cared to, because of the rabble and the age of many of the "flicks"— example: "The Lives of a Bengal Lancer."

During the day recorded music and Bob Hope and other programs were broadcast and filtered among the crap games to reach our ears with a great muttering and snapping of fingers.

One day a series of variety shows were given, consisting of a band (of musicians?), comedy and singing acts. Gave us a chance to glimpse the officers' lounge, if nothing else.

Recreation halls where one could smoke, listen to a "pianer" or write were furnished. With all the canteens available the lines still were utterly utter in length and slowness of movement. I did manage to get a carton of Hershey Almond Bars and some other things.

The best recreation, in spite of all this, came in visiting our friends (Charlie Fish, Marvin Goelke, Dick Gist and Sid Elliott) in other parts of the ship. At night we had quite a rumpus—what with people getting kicked out of their beds, clothing flying around, crap games getting tripped over, banjoes twanging—and laughter among the aforementioned friends.

Our chief source of annoyance and mockery came from the loud speakers posted all about. They were necessary in conveying information and war news and running the schedule—such as regulating chow formations. All day long the things drone out in harsh monotones. Especially irritating was the blast that broke into our sleep at six A.M. each morning. It was always the same: "ALL TABLE WAITERS AND CHOW LINE M.P.S REPORT TO THEIR RESPECTIVE MESS HALLS IMMEDIATELY —

It is needless to say — time did <u>not</u> drag.

VII

Bathing facilities were inadequate. We had a bathrub for our whole battalion. Frequently I'd sneak into a cabin and douse myself with salt water. It was rather strange and smelled a bit, but at least I felt clean and it soothed prickly heat.

Naturally the soap wouldn't lather, and the water usually wasn't just right, but I was satisfied. At one time I was running more salt into my pores than was coming out.

VIII

Outside the ocean roved in rhythmic, relentless rolls, flecked with lace-like caps of foam, straining in anguish at the wind that ruffled them, but retaining a delicate, blended texture, like a marble's core.

Up on the promenade deck I floundered in a chin high life preserver, on the edge of a similarly clad mass of humanity, waiting for a loud speaker to announce that the emergency muster was on. Every day at the same time this necessary boat drill took place. This, however, was the first time I had remained inside — instead of crowding on to a hatch on the forward deck.

Like a seal howling in a box of corn flakes, the loud speaker did spit, but it was abruptly cut off by a deafening "A-TEN-HUT!", and soon a meticulously dressed British Officer drifted by, two red crowns on his square shoulders wavering before my glazed eyes like two cigarettes in the dark.

At rest again, I saw a good looking first lieutenant stride over to one of the many square openings on the side.

"I love the water," he said. "I always want to hurl myself into it."

"Is that right?" I croaked, slowly backing into the crowd.

The lieutenent glowed. "Yes," he whispered, making a convulsive lurch up the side of the white wooden wall. "Sometimes I'm afraid to be alone in my room. I fear I may throw myself out the port hole."

I grinned hideously and managed to form an O with my mouth.

"Would you like to come with me?" he asked.

"Sorry," I gurgled, "I can't make it just now, but I have a friend who'd be glad to go with you . . . You stay right here—I'll be back in a jiffy."

I surged into the mob, struggled and at last unraveled myself from their humid presence. I found Fanset and dragged him with me, explaining I had a friend I wanted him to meet.

As we neared the open window my heart leapt. The lieutenant was not there!

Fanset sniffed. "Who did you want me to meet?" he inquired dubiously.

"No one. No one at all." I gasped . . . He'd have been happy, I thought, if I were with him. . . .

Outside the ocean still tossed and heaved, surrounding me with its salty breath. A billow of foam ripped itself from beneath the bottom of our ship and exploded outward, throwing its gnarled, twisted fingers into grotesque patterns. And when it finally disappeared in the crest of a sun-specked oily swell, it looked like a tiny silver bar. . . .

IX

The rumble grew and spread like a roar, even though it was supposed to be a whisper. Very soon we were rushing upward, crowding to the rail, feeling the spray and looking out. I wonder how so much excitement can be caused by a little four-letter word.

IN ADDITION

Sorry this got dirty—couldn't be helped. In order to avoid unnecessary mis-interpretation, I've made the following notes on the various episodes:

   I.   Right! It refers to us.
   II. Being in the army spoils everything. Nothing much impresses me.
VIII. I said not one word about the Lt. jumping in the water—nor intended to convey that impression.
  IX. Come now—it starts with "L" and ends with "d".

I didn't mention fish—but people said they saw a whale and dolphins —I didn't.

P.S.

THE CENSOR IS A BRAVE MAN—

BY THE WAY—

ALKA SELTZER IS GOOD FOR

HEADACHES

ENGLAND
AUGUST 1944

2

A Stand-by Sentinel: England and Brittany, August–December 1944

I was a dead-pan escort for two lady spies.

August 1944

Indian Summer

Sunday-in-England

Anthony Smith—a lil English boy from a nearby town is in our tent—We have a steady bunch of brats visiting us—(which we enjoy)—The first night on the field I slept in a pup tent—and was the warmest I've been in England —The scenery was magnificent—a brilliant yellow patch of mustard greens— gleamed far off—I climbed atop a monstrous hill—at the very peak was a rugged clump of trees—inside I saw shadows dance on the green carpet swirling round the trees—Everything was burnished with green—even the trunks—thick with moss—the whispering and the swishing and the solitude was unbelievable—

You've never seen such landscaping as they have in England—It's so orderly and varied you'd think it was posing—Usually the only things that break the smooth skyline are spires—mass movement of sheep—like a flow of white lava—moving in slow unison to the throaty bark of their tender patient sheep dog—WE NOW PAUSE TO ALLOW THE READER TO YAWN, GAPE AT REALITY AND MUNCH A CRUMPET . .

Funniest English sight—a huge wooly monster of a dog dragging its master down the road—Many people wear glasses . . all black-framed!

Sitting on the hillside—squinting thru the fog—we learned to recognize enemy uniforms, ranks—and watched demonstrations of tactics, habits and drill—In the afternoon we were given a chance to fire enemy weapons

I was glad I had three blankets that night—I slept on the ground—and I mean slept! In a farm yard I saw corn growing, the first I'd glimpsed in England. I sat down next to a goat. He was a friendly creature—but definitely not a conversationalist—

August 13, 1944

ENGLAND

V-MAIL

Relax, mama, I am gurgling with health!

From what I've seen of this island, I can truly say I loove it—it is beautiful, neat, and comfortable with age—The sight that impressed me most was a strip of green, rolling "Down," separated into halves by a road—On one side were hundreds of lambs, identically marked with black heads and black legs—On the other side of the road were hundreds of lambs, identically marked with white heads and white legs!

August 15, 1944

ENGLAND

Women have taken over the railroads and don't do too bad at that—Naturally, gambling and card games were in full sway (with the coach) but I preferred to gaze at the scenery and ramble in low tones with a certain T. Walters (Baltimore, Md.)—When I could see no longer, and the blackout went into effect—I wolfed one of my K rations and turned to the novel I now consider my favorite: "My Son, My Son"—

Sunday morn in England

Over here there is no race problems—Negroes are accepted as readily as whites—They even go to dances with white girls—Somehow—the average man in our outfit can't bring himself to understand or tolerate this—maybe I'm different—

August 30

ENGLAND

London Bridge didnt fall—neither did my spirits—I guess I'm kinda lucky—
I did see all the sights—I did have a wonderful time—in London—
  "Sutton's" is the name of a famous horticultural garden outside of London.
From the beautiful simplicity of the flowers we rolled into Paddington Station
—Large and leering—I had ridden with Tsgt Flynn, T-Sgt Turner, Tsgt
McIntyre—Pfc Jacobs & Pvt Sizemore—twas with the latter three I toured
and thoroughly enjoyed myself.

**We contend with tea, taxis, and the blackout—survey bomb damage, mount
stairs inside the dome of St. Paul's Cathedral ("seemingly spared by the blitz")—
all the dizzy way to the top—as if to match the wartime city's energy and
perseverance; relax at theaters, sample horse meat ("We ate the dessert despite
the whinny"), and finish with not quite a flourish chatting uneventfully with
ladies of the night.**

[undated]

Schones wetter nicht wahr?

  Well, it is here—Pleases me because I've had wet clothes piling up all week
—now they can dry—In about an hour and a half I'll be leaving on a pass—
tell you what 'appens tomorrow.
  Yesterday the mail call was halted by rain—and never was resumed—so I
cant refer to anything in yor letters (if any)
  The picture you see enclosed was taken on the spur of the moment—
otherwise I would have had on pressed khakis—my own rifle belt—and <u>my</u>
rifle—comprenez vous?
  The other two good pictures show (1) Big Ben and Abe Lincoln's Statue—
Houses of Parliament & Westminster Abbey are off to the right (can't be seen)
. . . in a previous letter I mentioned the "majestic simplicity" of the Abbey. I
meant majestic complexity—(2) St Paul's Cathedral—The cross as I said is
bright gold—the dome (outside) is green—

I was somewhat saddened at being put on a detail yesterday—but quickly
changed my mind as the day wore on—True—we worked a bit in the
morning loading boxes—or unloading them as the case may be—Later on
we got on trucks and drove to different towns—some quite far away—to

pick up supplies—All I had to eat during the afternoon (after a big lunch) were 3 cans of "C" rations—6 ripe tomatoes, half a box of dried prunes, 1 qt grapefruit juice—The reason for this was extra rations which the Sgt said we could have if—We could have carried more junk along but had no more room in our pockets—besides I already had crackers, cookies, and 11 candy bars back at camp—another guy in my tent had a can of fruit cocktail & two cans of tomatoe juice—So when I got back I helped get rid of that and a box of stuff Fanset had from the States—including cookies, rolls, and cake—It was then time for supper—so I hurriedly finished and went for stew, tomato sauce—bread—etc BURP

But coming back to the afternoon's festivities—I got a chance to go thru an old monk's abbey—one of many found in England—This one was 700 years old—and looked it—We saw the rooms and studio & sleeping quarters that the monks used—The grounds around the Abbey are still in good condition and are brightened with flowers—and believe it or not—a magnolia tree!

Back 'ome I showered and washed clothes—finished as the Co returned from a 3 hr—10 mile march!!!

August 1944

ENGLAND

Co A 376 Inf APO 94

Thursday morn—

[postcard]

In the fog this morn—I had a chance to drill the squad—I gave some flanking movements a bit too fast—causing eleven helmets to spin off and whirl away —with the result that the other platoons dived to the ground—thinking they'd seen buzz-bombs—

[undated]

IN ENGLAND

I've never weighed myself in England—and probably never will—The reason —Scales are made out in stones & pebbles—insert a pence and I see an amazing figure of 7 or 10 ??—

With a bit of time at my disposal — I'm finally doing what I wished to do at School (after I graduated): learn a foreign language —

At night in the tents with the rain beating down — we had fun just talking — No doubt you are getting mail as irregularly as me — But be patient — it'll come —

By the time you get this — many things will have happened on the Western Front — We get news but mostly "British — biased" —

Still working at the USO?

Cheerio — Ol' girl —

Located at Pinkney Park, near Sherston, Wiltshire, England, our regiment had trained, mainly in hedgerow tactics. On September 6, we left blacked-out Southampton on the HMS *Cheshire*, bound for an unknown destination in France.

September 12

A PEACEFUL EVENING IN FRANCE

A year ago today I had just glimpsed Fort Snelling — and was tasting my first army food — In my latest move we left the English camp by foot — carrying oversize packs — It was night — Somehow I reached the train — At our port we moved into a large warehouse to wait for loading — On ship — Hindus and Indians made up the working personnel — They jabbered continually and made huge sums of money from the gullible Americans — by selling candy bars — haircuts, milk . . Voyage was okay — frequent squalls kept us running down the hatchways — ashore — the heavy packs pulling down on our backs and shoulders — It was the hardest hike we ever attempted — marched over 7 hours! The country has the same green fields filled with cow dung as in England — Only the hedge rows are higher and thicker —

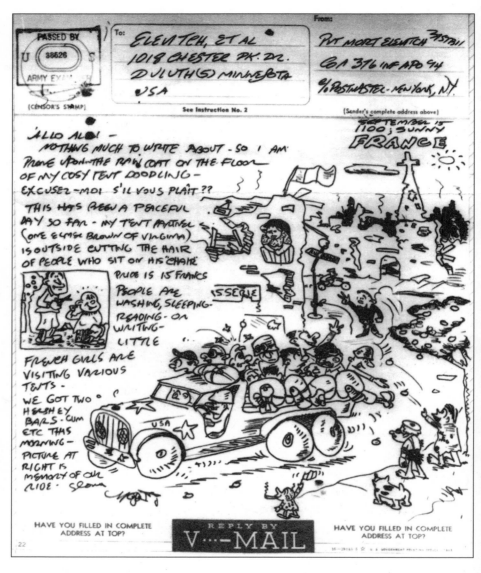

September 14, 1944. "The French people evidently haven't smiled in a long time. I did come all this way for a definite reason and now the time has come to do more than talk about it."

September 17, 1944

A SURPRISING SUNNY SUNDAY

FRANCE

'Allo all:

We've made our final move and are now situated near our scene of action*—
However my latest experience has been rather fast and a bit unusual—At this
moment I am seated in the shady back yard of a French merchant—in a busy
French town— ..

Sadly enough—this is only a temporary job—We are special guards for
the colonel and his regimental command post—Since the four of us (of the
original twelve) are posted in town—we moved our stuff in this morning—
just had lunch—chickens and cats putter around—once in a while soldiers
with steel helmets and rifles open the squeeky gate and stroll thru the yard—
I can see church steeples and chimneys above the roof tops—all magnificent
examples of French architecture—

My duties are not bad—we are on two hours and off six—I go on first
shift at eight thirty in the morning—This morning we were assigned to our
special posts—and the routine continues—until other arrangements are
made and we join our companies—somewhere near the front—

On duty this morning I was bothered by a persistent woman who wanted
to wash my clothes—but I'm afraid I'll never be able to pry them off—A
general said good morning to me, but I didnt find out who he was—for in
good military fashion—I was staring straight ahead, at present arms—

One trigger-happy guard the other night did some heavy blasting—After
the smoke and rubble had disipated—something soft and warm slithered
down the rifle barrel on to his quivering fingers—Shakily, the guard struck a
match and discovered it was the remains of his muzzle cover—

Au revoir

Mort

*Probably Heric, near Nantes, in Brittany. The division's first combat mission was to contain
pockets of Germans in and around the coastal towns of Lorient and St. Nazaire.

Sept. 18, 1944

F RANCE

'Allo Mama:

Just came off duty—the first shift of the special guard assignment—We are
nicely settled in the quarters of Monsieur (I shall use an alias) Drubble—
When we speak to him we roll the first syllable—like a Scotchman
(Ddrrr-ubble) causing the jolly-moustached old man to break into a hearty
hee-haw—our conversation is limited but we are getting along satisfactorily—
especially with their daughter who teaches us many things—The old man
runs a blacksmith shop while the wife and daughter operate a restaurant—
needless to say we have plenty to eat—

Madame insists on bringing us fresh bread (du pain) butter (du bur) and
eggs (du oefs)—she also heats water for us to shave in—naturally I make her
take money—and we help them clean up the yard—and carry things—they
are tremendously happy to have us after living under the Germans for four
years—The Nazis raided their garden and forced them to cook—Many other
things were done by the Jerrys—which I've seen and heard about—but will
not mention at this time—

Right now I'm sitting in the sunny back yard—Got a loaf of bread inside
steaming hot! (O mei wee!) Take a few slices when I go to chow and mail this
soon near the white chateau looming behind me—No one watches over the
four of us—We're on our honor to keep the guard going according to schedule
—WHAT A LIFE!

Most people wear wooden shoes to work in—They seem rather burdensome
—particularly while riding a bicycle—Usually the rider carries a pack on the
bike or back—or steadies a pitcher or cup in one hand—It is not unusual to
see whole families roll by on bikes—The little ones are delighted to see the
Americans—and are not bashful in asking for cigarettes!! French hats are just
as ridiculous as ever—resembling steam shovels—fish fins and what not—

Slong

later .. —

. . . Never have I seen a Frenchman with an umbrella or raincoat (unless it's
G.I. issue)—They plod along bareheaded, little children splash behind—A girl
might pause under a hedge row, while her boy friend stands on the road,

holding up her bike—The farmer drags his cow among the grain, sits under it, contentedly chewing bread and gulping cider . . .

Gertrude Stein said "The French are more spiritually minded" than the Americans—Actually they seem too stupid to realize there is no need to suffer the many inconveniences they contend with daily—Give a Frenchman a bar of soap, and he'll prob'ly set to work to carve a horse out of it—His dog eats the wasted chips—both are happy.

Sept. 21

France

'Allo mama:—

With the reappearance of the Luftwafte (such as it is) we got orders to dig slit trenches—after hacking away in solid shale for hours—I've almost completed mine—I got a few fine points on sculptery, as all the work was done with a pick—the shovel was merely used to remove the debris—

Three Germans who surrendered were brought in yesterday. One of them, a blond eighteen year old youth wearing the bright red striping of a cannoneer on his gray uniform, sat in the rear of a jeep, sullen and silent. He had given up because he was "tired of fighting"—an elderly jerry—valuable because of the vital information he knew, was anxious to "go to America and prepare a home for himself and [his] wife"—The story of their surrender is brave and daring—but details can not as yet be told, since it would involve revealing a clue to my location—

Sept. 22

'Allo all—

The Sgt. of the Guard told me last night that we were officially known as "The Regimental Commandant Guard"—(I say, fancy that, wot)

Had a fair shower yesterday noon—under the filtered sunlight of a secluded forest spot—felt wonderful—later I washed some of my filthy clothes—went to a well to draw a bit of clear water to rinse them in—Being very careful I tied my steel helmet to the hook on the chain and lowered away . . . Somewhere below the surface of the earth is a steel helmet with net attached—Fine thing—no steel helmet and in combat too—However—the army is very conscientious about replacing equipment lost in battle—My helmet should come in next week.

Had some fun last night teaching a small French boy English—he finally could go thru a whole sequence: "What is your name"—"My name is Jack"—"How are you"—"Fine thank you"—Jack has brought me fresh peaches and grapes—also wine & cider to the boys—he also acts in the capacity of booking agent for various mademoiselles in the vacinity—

Been hearing more examples of German fiendish cleverness—They've been known to drive right up to the gate of a cp* in a captured American vehicle—now they've been putting booby traps on our booby traps at night—Our men attempt to disarm our devices the next day—and are blown up for their trouble. We sometimes wonder if all the civilians & Free French wandering around here <u>are</u> what they seem to be—

I imagine it's safe to tell you the Free French are working with us here—at my last post—I was bothered all day long by a stream of them wanting gas for their noisy European cars—"Attendez" I'd say (for all I know, they are still doing same)—

Sept. 29, 1944

France

'Allo Mama:

Sittin' near a fire, a-lis'nin to the singin' of the water in a pot, and the cracklin' of the embers as they flutter in the flames—(a la Jesse Stuart). Came off duty at the crisp hour of 7 A.M., ate a measly breakfast of grapefruit juice, pancakes, bacon, cream of wheat—orange marmalade & butter & coffee—washed, shaved with precision steel Gilette Blue Blades exclusively bringin to you again this year the famous sports events of the nation, namely the world series, torridly described by dynamic Red Barber—with comments by Bob Elton, major pugilistic events, and the colorful Orange Bowl football game at Miami, Florida, New Year's Day, faithfully called by the one and only Ted Husing, hung out the blankets and here I am—

Gott holt of a lovely booklet—"Long, Long Ago" by A. Woolcott—the last literary work he (almost) completed before his death—The stories are all related in Woolcott's sincere, inimitable style—furnishing mucho enjoyment—especially since any piece of reading matter is appreciated at this time—

Plowing out of my tent at 4 AM. this morning, I fumbled around buttoning

*command post

my clothes, fastening my rifle belt—and was somewhat disgruntled to find my helmet would not fit—Blearily I removed the headpiece and peered inside—I nearly had kittens—As a matter of fact, I did have one—all curled up and sound asleep in the helmet—

October 2, 1944

FRANCE

Fear Drosh [brother]:

. . . the knowledge of a few casualties took the edge off the 'clever' letter I had intended to plaster on these pages—but bravely forward: Your first big air-mail letter came yesterday . . I had no idea any of my letters from England were "Warm and natural," mainly because it was never warm and I was never natural. The reason they prob'ly seemed better than average—is because I didnt have the time to pollute them with my feverish imagination—instead—described what I saw. If I do write a book—I can say right now that it will never be about anything I saw or did in the army—Those letters are but substanciation to a dream—let them sweat in the drawer forever for all I care— . . Have no fear of my craving packages—All I want is letters (glorified as yours) photographs, good books and magazines and occasionally razor blades—I have no need for cigarettes—but I know many (now smoking butts) that could use them—I could use that picture you found in "Life"—as a pin-up—People keep pictures in peculiar places—wrist watches, rings, bracelets, cigarette cases—and false teeth! . . Anxious to hear all the commotion involved in starting college—I know you know best what I like in my letters—so come across—pliz

October 3

'Allo all:

Streaking over the highway with a gutteral roar, past scores of waving villagers, priests and farmers, drab and straight as the bicycles they pumped, terraced greenery and the irregular fingers of trees, a G.I. truck never became muddled as this sentence as it carried me and others to town . . —I was very much surprized to find a large city—full of fashionable modern homes, industrious rehabilitation projects, gay people, and even streetcars—diminiative yellow things, that screeched and groaned—much as the ones I used to know. Most of the bombed areas are concentrated in a few battered blocks—the scars are healing over however more rapidly than you'd think—stores and streets were crowded with people, animals, vehicles and allied servicemen—French poodles strutted along leading their masters by flashy leather leashes—Babies were wheeled about in streamlined carriages—the sidewalks were too narrow for the load—I became involved in one embarrassing situation edged against the wall—Finally I decided to enlist my slight knowledge of French—"Ex-cuz-ay-mwa"—I politely rattled off to an elderly lady while giving a slight jostling movement in the direction I wished to travel—I was plastered right back in my original position as she swept by without so much as a glance. I tried again putting more expression and feeling into my pronunciation—"EX-KOOS-EE-MUH-WAA" I whispered deploringly—clicking my teeth and motioning with my hands—No response—This ludicrous incident was now going to extremes—"OX-KOOZ-AY-MWA-SEEL-VOO-PLATE!" I bellowed, receiving the same negligable result. Floundering in exasperation, I somehow struck on what I believed to be the solution—I would try the Charles Boyer method (after all, Boyer always gets results with women)—I pulled down my eyelids over swimming dreamy orbs, attempted to slightly muss my stubby fuzzy locks, squeezed my adams apple until a vein began a convulsive throb at my temple, pursed my lips, and in a low, haunting basso murmured, "EX-CUZE-AY-MA-SEE-VOO-PLAY"—(I blew out the "ma" like a smoke-ring) . . Eyeing my fingers which were softly caressing my streaked rifle-stock, the buxom blonde on whom I was experimenting stabbed me in perfect English: "That's a hell of an act soldier, but I don't think you're one bit funny—why don't you get out of the way and let me by"—Gladly, gladly, I fled far away—and soon was once again droning at the castle moat with the other insects—

October 4, 1944

Dear Paw Paw

At long last I hit the jacqualine-pot, finding a store, where there was a kindly, unshaven monsieur—who offered to supply the necessary ration tickets—Before he left—he designated the two items I could purchase—For Burr I got a bow-tie—and would have done the same for you—but for the fact that the gentleman had stipulated a tie and a handkerchief—Well, a handerchief is nothing to sneeze at—So I took it—knowing you could not use it as a pocket decoration or utility—Instead I reasoned—you could best put it to good vantage by setting a picture or vase on it—You might use it on the back of a chair—or as a last resort display it at half-mast in the event of a national calamity—

'Allo Maw-Maw:

Slicked up and clean with fresh clothing from my duffle bag—I was happified to learn—two morns ago—that a truck was going into (tut-tut-tut—mustn't tell you know) Anyhoo—was a nice big city—with 'lil streetcars scooting around—Rightaway it was evident rebuilding was progressing with no intention of retaining the ideas of old France—I saw some of the most beautiful fashionable homes that I've seen in any European city—The people had bright, modern clothes—and of course—nothing can surpass the astonishing hats—Babies were pushed along in stylish streamline carriages—Blotched and scarred was the center of the city—which had not escaped the bombs of the boche—

October 5, 1944

Fear Drosh:

Instead of repeating everything I've told Maw-maw & papa in the last two hours—I'll condense my version to youse—In short I: went to a loovely beeg city—NANTES . . Had one wonderful time—but got wet (and later cold) Groggily arose the next morn—ripped open a V-mail—gasped and shuddered at the glaring masterful face of Agamemnon Ulk*—

French keeds are quick to adopt the "funny book"—I am sending you one —let me know what I was laughing at last nite

Oct. 13, 1944

FRANCE

Fear Drosh—

OBSERVATION AND CONCLUSIONS AFTER
TWO-AND-ONE-HALF HOURS WITH A FRENCH WHORE

Sorry—no need to get aroused—Mohr-ton is still the same old innocente—still the skeptic of man's joys—But he has had another experience—which—fortunately—filled idle time—his stomach—and kept him out of the rain—I have just completed—this windy afternoon—a further expedition to the city of Nantes—still seeking our goodwill, our generosity—and our money—The

*The presidential candidate we'd invented.

French people think more of their daily recreation (well maybe not more) than the hurry and scurry derived from the modern business world—thus— the Nantes stores provide a 2 1/2 hour rest period—commencing at noon . .

So it was in the rain I met this T/4 John (last name unimportant) . . We were looking for a restaurant—It is just then—that a much too blonde decides she is going our way—and steers us to an empty cafe down a gloomy side street—In same she proceeds—with ample ale (or rather wine) to give us the sob story and in fair English too—shows us pictures (when she was brunette and in love with a gay Parisian goggling under a beret) . .

It is quite evident that she is not unsatisfied with the tall one she pecks at and clings to opposite me—("Babb-ie"—she calls me) John asked her where she learned to speak good English—I was delighted by her frank answer— "I learned it one night"—she also declared her blonde gravel gerties were camoflage necessary to her business—in all—she wasn't too bad to look at— especially when reflected in the misty palour of the liquid in the glasses—She had the dainty black dot of a birthmark (a la pencil) on her left cheek—The ruby red of the quivering lip—The finely clipped eyebrow—and the blue eye which succumbed to the blearited glaze of a "spirited" daze—

But to the restaurant—and then <u>through</u> it—to a small back room—quiet reserved—complete with French art (naked women smoking in various poses) and a well-equipped bar—boasting a prune pit mouth and a pigeon eye—all wrapped in white coat—He served us white wine—and slowly—like the pieces of a shipwreck floating down a river—brought in our dinner— flippantly ordered by Helene Surget—(the woman) who had consented to dine with us (after much persuasion)—I enjoyed the ring of tomatoes he dropped before us first—and the sickly brown peaches that accumulated at the end—

All morsel of matter was devoured by lively Lucy—Once she came over to me—and decided after my reluctance at being called "Babb-ie" to address me as "mon cherie"—a considerable improvement—But for John she had a great desiring for the flesh as it were—she nipped the nape of his neck—and he irresponsibly allowed her to peck his cheeks—She had the uniqueness to suggest she was <u>cold</u>!—But he only called her a devil—repeating she was no good for him (a former English teacher married 7 years) . .

By the time I left them she had given him a hotel address, had assured him she wasn't ticklish by guiding his hand in the right places—and was halfway thru the second bottle and a bit of song—Coffee and brandy were on the way—but I paid my share—bade them bon chance and smiled out the door—

Enough! On to your books—

October 20, 1944

Fear Drosh

On a postcard I sent you I mentioned sompin 'bout a haircut and shave I watched—the patient slips his arms into a white gown—which is draped over the body—He sits in the chair facing a mirror—wash basin and accessories—My barber was a frail little man with slick black hair—His eyes were flies floundering in dabs of cream, never quite surmounting the ridge that was his nose—in his priestly robe he moved like a white saint, cutting smoothly—To administer a shave he used no series of hot towels to soften the skin—Only a vigorous—drawn out application of bubbling lather—flowing out of a tall silver cylinder— . . . Then in quick flashing slashes the barber removed the beard—seemingly the most unimportant maneuver of the entire operation—The customer is then allowed to rinse to wash the remaining goo off his face himself—As he settles back again—he is caught in a stifling stream of scented liquid spattering from a syphon bottle—Thoroughly doused and dripping—he gets no time to relax—as his head is rolled and molded by strong fingers—The flesh becomes a glistening pink after five minutes of rubbing—This necessitates the application of powder—which is gathered by a fluffy white ball—The powder is permanently ground in as grease is added with the finger tips—The befuddled individjidool in the chair next receives a haircut—Then like a bootblack—the barber slaps on polish—brushing it in until he achieves a blinding intensity—Soon the entire job is completed, the beret is eased on to the skull, the check paid, and the customer staggers out the door—Meanwhile the next fool (twas myself) is startled to his senses as a bell is clanged in front of his face. Too bad I didnt get to see a shampoo demonstration—but the shave alone took an hour—so I was satisfied—

"Proclamation" is the second of three playful letters to my brother, the college freshman. It pledges fraternal fidelity and is based on a German or local emblem/insignia (banner? plaque?). The first letter, dated October 1, 1944, redresses in pure Dada a slighting remark Burr had evidently received: "I have never chanced to harken to the melody and lotus blooms radiating from your gentle script—my dear brother—my mottled, incorrigible face fondly stroked the parchment"; and the third, undated, is "Consternation," omitted here, a "true story" but a self-mocking burlesque: "A cat gave its interpretation of Pagliacci in the dismal hours of the night, sending echoes bounding banshee-like down the silent streets of the village . . Cringing at my guard post . . ." This staunch guard is approached by two mysterious strangers and after numerous mental contortions discovers, through the intervention of a general, that they only want a match.

— PROCLAMATION —
— of Les Philadelphia —

BE it hereafter known to all concerned, that inasmuch as
THE GRAND SEAL of DROSH and ELEVATE
Is an emblem of emminence, it shall be treated accordingly, and shall be reverently interpreted as follows to wit:

WHEREAS the two black eagles of the family, DROSH and ELEVATE, are outstanding in the centre, firmly affixed by the inseparable bond of tar and feather — each facing the direction of the LIGHT he seeketh, but seeketh in vain, for in the empty candle sticks each clutches, there kindles not so much as a spark — their ears have ceased producing wax.

WHEREAS the castle above represents their CROWNing achievement; each segment a stage in their strange and varied lives: ANÆMIC, MORONIC, IDIOTIC, and HYDRAULIC. (the last, possibly, for water on the brain) The castle remaineth curved in nature — they never could get anything straight anyway.

WHEREAS the colour scheme of things is thus:

RED is for the bloodshot that rattles in their eyes.
BLACK is for the polish that shines their evil mind.
GREEN is for the rawness of their words and vicious lies.
GOLD is for the heart, which in them you will not find.

BLUE Represents their mothers worry, and all the sighs and tears.
SILVER forms the blade or bullet each haunted brother fears.

FRANCE
OCT. 5, 1944

93

October 29

FRANCE

Dear Little Brother:

Two shocks came in letters from Paw Paw & you yesterday—the sale of the store and the apparent absolute zero temperature of your early enthusiasm. As usual I must attempt to cheer up the family—and myself—Right now I'm rather cramped—Laying on my stomach in the tent right after eating chow in the rain which still patters. Frankly—I am now enjoying the best life I have had in the army—although it may end soon or even in a few hours [special guard detachment]. You can't imagine how revelating it feels to be left alone for awhile instead of being led and pushed around all day—the way it used to be—You too are on your own—now—managing your own daily schedule—although under vastly constrasting circumstances—By now you may have found the companionship you desired—If not—then I dont need to tell you that it is your own fault—I never have been in a formal fraternity nor found it necessary to do so in order to get around—have fun—and be on the inside—as it were—and yet I have frequently found myself wondering—'member the mood I was in when I came home on furlough?—True I had the gang of Fanset—Ellicott—Fish etc but something was lacking—Now we're all separate—

The first dawning came on my trip to London. There I was with four fellows each of whom had interests widely different from my own. Right off I decided to go more than halfway—which I'd stubbornly refused to do in the F E E combination—Before I knew it—the others had satisfied their desires—Burlesque show—pubs—Picadilly at night—and had turned to me for suggestions—It was I who directed the tour of the city—which three of them enjoyed—It was I who found the ice cream shop and Gay Paree Cafe—for which they were grateful—By the end of the second day—I was getting on intimately with guys I'd never hardly spoken to or matched up with before—it's been that way ever since—In spite of the delights sought out by many in Nantes [whore houses] I remained aloof and yet had a wonderful time—Take the T-4 "John" incident for example—And I actually made the extreme sacrifice of eating meat just so I could hang around with "eating" Ellicott and F—I realize you want the companionship of many—you arent bashful—but just lack the spark due to your sense of modesty and self respect—Well, if Mohr-ton could manage it—you can—If you have to miss a concert once to do something with a guy—do it—Dont ever miss another concert—but show him or her you have enough consideration of his feelings to be interested in what he might want on that occasion—

Now PawPaw has given up the store—the only stable thing we had to back us up—It'll never be the same with the little white-fringed bald man bobbing about—grinning—making fun of Finns—Eh—Duluth Hardwaring over the phone—uh—Duh-whating with a blank gaze—irritating sweet Evelyn—cynical and biting—enraged and amused at his brawling boys—Loudly kissing "baby" Franklin—Swearing at selling nails as he tried to close the store—buttoning his trousers in front of lady customers—

Paw Paw was small—but like all great people—was a legend—he served the poor people—he continued hackneyed letters and worn-out methods scorned by modern business—The fishing license sign forgotten in the window thru the winter—The fourth of July flag—gathering dust in September—

PawPaw will soon be forgotten—and the "Store" will grow and modernize and carry on its miserable but proud existance—

At least we're really on our own—I am still held down—but for a year at least you are free to enjoy yourself—but you'll have to find the people to fill that vacant corner you have—Go ahead and do what you like—but make the best of it—

I'm now leaning on my knees—isn't raining anymore. Candles in here have been going for hours—No show this aft—Guess I'll have to finish this "better-than-a-book"—[*Valley of Decision*] read the thing if possible—it can be stretched to pattern itself after our lives—"The Store"—Scott's Steel Mill—"Claire" might even be you or me—

You dont offend me when you write letters—"Consternation" had those abominal phrases because they were what I wished to express—dozens of words roam around in my mind but unlike you I dont know they're meaning or spelling—why not SEND ME A <u>GOOD</u> <u>SMALL</u> DICTIONARY??

Long letters must make you feel I'm having it awful easy—I am someone who had to have this guard job—But when I go back to the front don't expect nothing but sorrowful things <u>you</u> used to send me—

Slong

Mort

Afterthot

The yellow paper was wrapped around my German candles —
    This other letter is from Fanset — Hope you can read it — He — easier and far
more successfully than I — went thru the conceited — embarrassed — not being
able to dance — stage easier than I — Notice how he mentions his lowering of
morals — He never used to drink or smoke (I dont yet) but now has made
the plunge in order to be a "regular" with the gang he went to Nantes with —
(I DONT SUGGEST YOU DO THIS) Notice the discreet mentioning of my absent
restraining force he used to depend on. Omigod been writing my arm to
stiffness and I have to write Paw Paw yet!

AMERICAN RED CROSS

October 17, 1944

Dear Mort,

Found your letter waiting for me when I got back from town last night. In my
dazed condition I wasnt able to make much out of it. Just got done reading it.
Things are beginning to get clear now.
    I should think you would be able to get to town more often. I've been there
both times on a Mon. & the stores arent open at all on Monday! What a
country!
    Would like to have seen you in operation with the blonde. [Helene] Must
have been a tough situation. These French women can be pretty forward, if
that's a strong enough expression.
    I had quite a time yesterday . . We visited all the whorehouses. I've lost a lot
of my high morals this past year, but I dont find it especially hard to overcome
the temptations afforded by one of France's specialists trades. Certainly did
have a time inviting the interests of the Fifi's & then saying Au Revoir . . . Youd
think all these women would begin to look alike to you, but each one stands
out distinctly in my mind. I never thought I would enjoy watching wholesale
debauchery but instead of disgust I found myself amused & interested (but
not physically). Who can tell, my next step from Champagne and Cognac
will be upstairs in a whore house! Heaven forbid. What I need is a certain
influence to protect me. I used to know such a person but he's not with us
anymore.

Guess you know as much about what goes on here as I do. You've probably heard all the rumors. I hope the one about the 302nd is true. I'd sure like to see Ellicott again, wouldnt you?

Regards, Jack

October 29, 1944

— France —

Dear Dad —

Yesterday I was shocked by two letters, one announcing Burr's apparent drop of enthusiasm to absolute zero — and the other telling of the proposed sale of the store — I've already sent off nine pages — trying to cheer up the young'n — By now the whole deal is prob'ly over with — nevertheless — I am still dismayed at the prospect of having no more "store" — The old familiar stock of odds & ends to look forward to — for your sake I am glad to be rid of a menace to your well-being — and yet I know how you hated to give it up — it was the one remaining thing you had left after we departed — The store has always possessed you — it would have been a fine thing if you could have possessed it — By that I mean — have it working for you thru someone else's management and worry — But you know more about what you did than I — still I wish we could have had something — stable — lasting — built up to fall back on — in case our wandering interests folded up — You were undoubtedly right when you said we showed too slight an interest to warrent your keeping it up — But then too — remember how young and unsettled we both were — never satisfied — never content — typical of most boys approaching college age — I feel that some arrangement might have been worked out to preserve the business you slaved so hard to build and establish — It isnt the idea of the money so much — as the basis of something for us to do — in case it became necessary — Burr had suggested the store as a jumping off place — a "retreat" to burn up energy while I was attempting to write or get started in some such unstable profession — But now for the first time we realize we are on our own — must make our own life as you did — now what is important is your future — I cant imagine you idle for one minute — I'm waiting to hear what you have decided to do to occupy your time — I know how you love to putter around — and beautify our home — will this be enough? — As long as I am able — I will keep letters pouring in — I was just thinking that a trip — although I know how you feel about such things now — would be beneficial — maybe to California — We had always planned to make one together. But there is no reason why you can't blaze the trail—so you'll know where to take me whenever the time comes—if I ever get off this continent—I'll be content to remain in the western hemisphere—I assure you—With winter coming up—an excursion—which you never had time to do—might be wise—The house could be kept up—It may sound ridiculous but mom could keep an eye on it—after all you must admit she can at least see that things are kept fresh and clean—Of all the homes I've seen now in half the world I think I'd rather reside in the place you had so much pride in—"The Big House"—I know you'll keep it—the walks in the raw air now—along the blvd—must seem strange—when you know there'll be no rush to open the plate glassed door, turn on the light—and stamp upstairs to the office in the store—Remember that you have two unusual children—They have been molded in a rush—but from good stock—the circumstances under which we have lived and worked have seemed to build a wall about us—a closeness that was there but at times discouraging because of the struggles and troubles we encountered every day—Usually we gave the impression that we never thought you understood —but deep down we know that you understood far more than we did—It has been your giving nature that has backfired on you all along—even with your children, but I think you know how we admired you—and how we echoed your air of accomplishment—now although separated we will try to repay you through our thoughts and words if not by actions—Yours has been a hard life but you may be sure you have given your boys—in spite of them—valuable traits and common sense and broadmindedness which few others are fortunate enough to inherit—But still I am unscarred—still I am the vicious red head who climbed up on your knee to hear the funnies—

Mort

'Allo maw-maw

I sent pawpaw an article explaining proposed army plans for the army of occupation—If I have to stay here—I'd like to travel and study—But first a month at home!!

FRANCE

'Allo Ma-Maw:

Again yesterday I rode to Nantes—where I had one el goode time—arriving early, I decided to take a shower—which I did—in a schoolhouse—well equipted with little individual shower nooks and duckboards — The bldg guarded by a concrete pillbox, was formerly occupied by the boche — Then FFI — and now us'ns — comprende?

October 31, 1944

halloween

[BRITTANY, FRANCE]

Dear Mom,

Two nights ago I was a dead-pan escort for two lady spies — A soldier of the FFI,* formidable tho mild — appearing — had marched them, shivering but hauty into our CP — Since it was necessary to deliver the women to proper hands for interrogation, a truck was selected for the purpose — with a guard — which happened to be me —

Before we left, however, Chance — my former fellow guard from "A" Co. had jumped aboard to squeeze down behind the ladies' bicycles and bags — which we also hauled — The last passenger was to prove our most valuable one — Louie — a French interpreter who finally decided to come along —

Of the two girls — one was blonde and nervous — the other dark and well rounded — was worried but maintained her good looks with hurried dabs of lipstick applied by a cigarette light — glowing in the chill interior of the truck — No one talked very much — Once in a while Louie would lean forward to shout directions to the driver to send the truck careening down the bumpy — gloom-spattered roads. I thought how easy it would be for the dark girl to grab his knife if she wished — Occasional rain lashing the canvas added to the sober recklessness of the ride, causing the girls to cringe with cold in spite of blankets and jackets we'd allotted them.

At the town we sought, dreary and deserted to outward appearances — Louie took complete command — and after several futile searches down twisted streets succeeded in locating the CIC —

Once again we acted the chaperone roll herding the tense girls into a high, well-lighted hall, fascinating with the most splendid examples of taxidermy

*French Forces of the Interior — having previously fought in Italy — consisting of remnants of the French army, new recruits, and resistance fighters from all nations, whose most conspicuous leader was General de Gaulle. Supplied and trained by the Americans, they nevertheless in our area were independent, seeking (and finding) confrontation with Germans (the *Boche*).

I have seen since Fields in Chicago — The walls were teeming with plaques — marked and dated according to the particular specimen — there were many heads of bores [*sic*], deer, wolves and an amazing ash-tray-stand — a grinning gopher-like animal-upright offering a tray — We settled ourselves in an elaborate room — rich with furniture, decoration, a blazing fireplace, and more trophys — even an albatross — and the "saw" of a saw fish — A young wall-eyed stubby Lt. told us that we were in the home of a millionaire naturalist, an adventurer who had made many exploratory expeditions and had hunted with a lust for knowledge rather than sport —

We removed our overcoats & field jackets to allow for the warmth — and quietly watched the stiff suspects at the table separating them from the experienced officers who would question them — We sat in the room while the FFI man was taken out for verification and facts of the story — which we, unfortunately, never did learn.

We did know that one girl — the blonde of course — was Polish — supposedly 35 — The other French and 17 — The ages must have been stretched — Only the fair haired one with the red face and morbid eyes had papers — The other had only scraps of letters and wrinkled cards to offer —

The final decision was to keep them overnight until further proceedings would substantiate or renounce their stories. We were to take the FFI to his command winter quarters for lodgings for the night. Shortly afterward we left — but not before an interesting discussion with an officer who informed us of his work — of the filtering of spies thru the lines to operate in Cafes — of the unfair hostility of the people toward foreign immigrants and German-speaking French —

In the gloom again we dropped off the bicycles and roared away. Fifteen minutes later I was surprized to find two more women spies crouching in our truck! They'd been waiting for us at FFI — dark — shifty-eyed — tattered mangy things — hunched and frightened — the type that leans against buildings, peers from doorways — and invites the foolish to "come along" —

Back we went to the CIC — who were more surprised than we were — "Everything happens at night" — they exclaimed.

We were in another room — a dining room — cheery smelling of food and wine and healthy effort of a good wife — we saw her — grey haired — smiling — feeding her own children and men of the CIC — and there hovering at the table edge were our first two black pidgeons — shaking but eager and hungry. Silently the 2nd two, lingering near the door, eyed the others — and meekly accepted glasses of wine — Being served to us by the family — who also brought chairs — as tho they were used to such outlandish interruptions in their evening meal — The roundup was completed — We said our thanks and turned away once more, closing the door on the room of strange occupants and full-mouthed departing remark of a little French Boy: " — G.I. Joes" —

November 15

Fear Drosh:

After nearly two months of luxury as far as the army goes, my good fortune came to an end as the order came down for a bunch of us to return to our companies — Yesterday I had gone jeep riding — returned and open mouthed found my tent torn down — so we set up a new post — a regular "chateau"! It was (and is) a wonderful thang — about 6 × 12 × 6 — We worked all day eager to make a good job of it — Sgt Porter comes around just as we finish — with the sad news — so for tonight at least we will enjoy our home — well lit with candles — Tomorrow I'll head back for some new experiences at the front — I guess I can be thankful for the past two months — From now on I'll try to be the well-known doughboy

Mort

Co A 376 Inf APO 94

November 30

(Republican Thanksgiving)

Dear Mom:

Your letters of Nov 2 and 14 were handed to me yesterday while I was eating chow with the third platoon — which I am now a part of again! — Moved out here yest morn in a jeep — Got assigned to the second squad — all day we worked on a hole for ourselves — dragging logs — hunks of tin and boards — Today we worked on another dugout — finished shortly after lunch — Talked a Free Frenchman out of a beautiful — thick — <u>warm</u> — jacket — The fur is all <u>white</u>! — Had a picture taken of me in it today — looks like an ermine cape! Kinda cool and sunny — blankets and clothes are airing — slept in a tent — had 3 guard shifts — pretty quiet just now — Mortar shells whistle over head occasionally — Others still pound and chop — fixing up their hole

"Sir, I need an order to fill hole."

December 4

Dear Mom—

Sittin' in one of the nicest holes I've seen—belonging to a machine gun crew
—For whom we're now acting as security—moved yesterday—my hole is
French made with a pine needle roof—okay but kinda low—Last night on
guard after I'd succeeded in piling on my field jacket—fur jacket—overcoat
and raincoat I nearly roasted to death—The FFI around here are same as we've
encountered—constantly bickering for cigarettes—chewing gum—chocolate

— and "cheek" chewing tobacco — Standing in our emplacement I "Bonjour" my two hours away — Washed my feet again today and changed <u>socks</u>! — had the last pair on since Thanksgiving — if it's nice tomorrow I'll wash my hair —

The day has been everything from cloudy to blinding — Now and then a black puff of smoke from a bursting artillary shell drifts up and dissolves — The pines and leafless skeletons of trees sway — Beneath them the lumpy hedgerows are bleak and speckled with moss and parasitic growths — In the roads and fields the mud and pasty pools persist — Such is the setting — At chow time it is good to sit around and gab and see familiar faces of those scattered about at different points on our front — reading "Skin and Bones" by Thorne Smith — Our tiny stove — which we use to heat water — coffee etc — was made in Albert Lea (Minn) — I'm getting tired of cleaning my rifle — then having it get wet again — gonna try to get a sten gun to supplement it —

December 8

Dear PawPaw

Two days ago I did make a deal and got me a nice sten gun — It is slightly under three feet long including the stock — Spent all day yesterday cleaning it — Now it will fire single or automatic — just by a slight pressure on the trigger — I have over 200 rounds of ammo left — and four magazines — The main advantage of my sten is that I can carry it around in the rain and not worry about my M-1 getting wet

December 10

Fear Drosh —

This room I'm in — it's almost like one of yours — except maybe for the six rifles, four sten guns, a pistol and a revolver — and the cartridge belts and packs and ammo bags — behind — six of us in here — all kids — with beds — German beds — hard metal straps to lay on — but I fixed mine with cardboard and paper and a folded shelter half — light in here too — only they flick on and off — Someone always foolin' around — Fixed up the socket last nite — French type light bulb with two tits — as "Boomer" said — nice place — we're in barracks — German barracks . . would have written you last nite but the sudden change from a damp hole to this palace caused the boys to let off steam — It all starts when blond — curly — "Eart" — "Whatsoever" Joe Sanniac [Sanniec], our new squad leader — began to fondle "Ruby" Costello — in bed next to mine — As he was "tearing her panties" a gradual onrush of humans descended — Soon the place was nothing more than a thrashing melee of heads—arms—and legs—Over and over they roll around the room—At this time I am merely lying serenely in my bed—On a shelf I have my toilet articles—toothbrush—tooth powder—soap—wash rag—shaving cream and razor—At least twenty times I pick up toothbrush—toothpowder—soap—wash rag—shaving cream and razor—Then Costellos head is bashed against a wall—K.O. (Otto) Kettler—a smooth fiend from Texas is giving the little one a grip upon his foot—At that moment Walter C. Taylor—dives in flourishing a cleaning rod—intending to administer a pro—Now all of us have just washed up—using a small gas stove—even Thomas "Carl" Walters—who is upon the floor—a mussed and sweaty mess—Even "Geetzy" Fogli joins us—working his bare bow legs thru the door ahead of his twinging nose—He is accompanied by my good good friend Hatleberg—slightly cognaced—Now Otto has appeared in a blue Nazi uniform followed by Joseph in a bobbing gold helmet with a glistening pointed peak—Otto decides to throw bayonets at Ruby—squint eyed and breathless in a corner—Jenkins and Bobby Murlin have somehow become entangled on the latter's bed—Dorman Brown is calmly writing letters on the table—on which Sgt Clarence Reimers—squats on his double-jointed legs—wool cap down over his ears—rabbit-skin jacket tickling his chin—squealing with delight—I simply moaned and worry about my rumpled bed—"It is 10 p.m." somebody yells—and everything suddenly subsides—I decide not to write a letter—besides I get none—same today—and have only sampled some popcorn saturated wit benzene from a cigaret lighter which someone sent Costello—This morn I flex my corrugated spine and look down at the little one—gruesomely twisted in a sleeping bag on his sagging bed—I ask if it will come out like tooth paste if I squeeze it—Then I put on my boots—I am on k.p.—I tread down the dim and soft floored hallway and go out into the rain—There I stand all day scraping dried blood out of cumbersome greasy pans—For breakfast we have crispy french-fried toast—corn flakes—bacon—This noon—breaded Pork chops—french fried pomme de terre—corn, bread, jam—pineapple chunks

—Came in here after breaking my back dumping slop in the sump—nearly suffocated—washed up—feel better—got rations—Bob and Otto and D.E. are playing blackjack—chewing gum—smoking—In an hour I'll be leaving for a movie—showers tomorrow—I hope—First change of clothes since Thanksgiving—We are in a rest area

A lovely
December 11, 1944

Dear madre —

I am seated on my bed in our room below an open window which admits a
cool breeze — it is sunny out — I can hear the blump blump — a volley ball
game — You might think we were in a regular college dormitory except for the
rifles, sten guns, pistols, cartridge belts and ammo bags hanging on the wall —
the six of us in here are all "kids" — 18 and 19! — We are in German barracks
— completely equipted with dim apartment-ish hallways — gorgeous tile
lavatoires and shower rooms (not useable however) — Last night we were
supposed to see a movie — unfortunately the sound broke down — Three
false alarms and the thing was called off. — Then followed the most amazing
thing — It all started when our new squad leader — a Chicago gunman named
Sanniac — made remarks about living in the wilderness in Canada — Soon we
were sprouting on archaeology — anthropology, genology and astronomy —
Even evolution, heredity . . physio chemistry — Sgt Joe was curiously silent
for twenty minutes — finally came up with an example of evolution — "How
come," says he "years ago girls of 18 were flat-chested — and now dey got a
turty-two inch bust?"

Our high-toned discussion went on til way after midnight . . This morning
we bundle up and trundle off on trucks to take a shower — my first since
Thanksgiving — Wot a ride! wot country side! Reimers just squeeked in wailing
"I couldnt sleep a wink last night" — Murlin gazes at the stove — Costello and
Walters have gone to town — I can hear the spu-whoom of shells someplace —
all our missing clothing and equipment is supposed to be replaced — you see,
ma — we are in a rest area goobye

December 13

G'morning —

Sad news comes — we'll have to fall out shortly for mine school — last nite
our gayest — truly spontaneous and unmitigated revelry — December 14 . .
When I last left off I intended to tell about the previous nite — I came in to find
a mild discussion on music — Spike Jones came up — "As Time Goes By" —
"Hotcha Chonia" — The door was now opening frequently — admitting sorted
astonished individuals — Costello was raking them in cordially — by now the
festivities were reaching the tension point of a Haitian fettish — "Hubert"
"Yogi" Reimers dived for my white jacket — dropped it over his cranium — in
the manner of English judges & began to conduct a seance — using the white

globe procured from the ceiling and the wan light of a flashlight to give it a milky glow — he screwed up his face — pushed down two buck teeth and imitated Porky Pig drowning in a rain barrel — People were bounding on the beds — everyone's blankets were jumbled in lumps on the floor table and wash basin .. The poor French were slandered as a vent for our troubles — Brown and Murlin became entangled in "ites" and "ians" — the method of addressing Minnesotans, Wisconsinites, Londoners etc — They were convinced that Parisians couldn't be called Parisites, since, as Murlin stated, that is a term applied to <u>all</u> Frenchmen —

In the town I journeyed to yesterday afternoon — Met a girl — she had learned English in China, French in England, and was now studying German in France! In town I liked the washing women on their knees — the urchins begging for gum — a popular magazine was advertising Goddard and Chaplin in "The Little Dictator" —

Finally got my sleeping bag — veddy nice — has a heavy gold zipper, which allows you to zip up into a cozy cacoon —

Now I'm again in my warm room — Outside's gray — but the glossy green and snappy red of the holly trees keep things far from sober —

December 14

Fear Drosh

Much fun yesterday — A German 88 opened up — You shoulda seen us oozing in the ground with much hurry — If you hear the shells eweeeeeeeee ski WHOUMP! — You're okay — If not .... — Later our artillary is commencing. Along with mortars — At such time I was peacefully writing to mama in a hole (I was in a hole) washed my hair this morning — got out lots of dandruff — Most peekoolyar — some of the dandruff was black and had wings — Showed Fantasia your last letter — He suggested I send you a potato masher (which I have — German model 43) so you could get the spuds to the right consistency or end your misery — I <u>did</u> tell papa I only wanted de sto' to "Fall back on" — I am in full accord with his plans —

December 15

G'Morning —

On guard last nite Walters and I had a chance to mutter dreamily — First on the subject of "pre-destination," as he calls it — referring to the process of "remembering you've done something before" altho' you've never actually

done it—such as meeting someone in a dream—and then having it happen—
It's hard to put a finger on but you "just know" you've experienced the
particular sensation—"somewhere" before—Then I consider something
higher than life—something developed differently and totally undescribable
in "life" terms—fascinating speculation—what—This inevitably leads to what
is it all for?—why?—and, consequently the end of our fevered whisperings—
Besides we must separate for a while—

At chow this morning—(FF toast—eggs—wheaties) "reverend" Moore
gropes in—glazed blue eyes misty. He is told the third platoon is guarding 57
Nazis they caught during the night—"Gawllee"—he murmurs, "body's liable
to get his throat slit 'round here"—

December 17

FRANCE

Dear NaOH:

Sunday—outside the sun is bright—Another breeze is cool—all the green
things are fluttering—Our closed door excludes all but the sound of Protestant
services resounding in the hall—Only Walters, Costello and I are in here—
Usually the place is crowded—last nite it was crowded—We talked about you:

HATLEBERG: Seems to be coming out of the adolescent stage—

WALTERS: Has he been drunk?

MORT: No

WALTERS: He ought to get good and drunk and dabble in the wicked—
ought to make a girl fall for him—Then ditch her—

MORT: He won't do it—

COSTELLO: If he's happy as he is, that's all that matters—Maybe he should
try to take out an older more intelligent girl—than he is—

MORT: He won't do it—If I suggested slop like that—It would only amuse
him—but anyday I'm expecting news that he made the plunge.

MURLIN: Your brother's like you—

REIMERS: HUH—Wut's he done?

BURNS: Draw my picture, Mort.

HATLEBERG: I remember one girl I wore myself out on one night before a
track meet.

JENKINS: What event were you in—the broad jump?

BURNS: Draw my picture, Mort

And so the conversation on you went on and on—and I came to the conclusion that such things come to a conclusion—Keep happy brother—just tell 'bout junk as you have been.

Got your razor blades some time ago—used one to trim my moustache (?) today

Had a party at 2 A.M. this morning—Cleaned up everything for general's inspection—only an idiot kid came in bringing mud—cross-eyed with snot running out of his nose and ears—"Allez-allez-btttrrt!" we told him—

Mort

December 19, 1944

NaOH*

We are now in the new area—occupying old barracks used by some of our troops in 1918—This morning we chipped our way out of our frigid sleeping bags, thawed out our toes—shortly departed for batallion medics to receive a shot— . . . Boomer just staggered in bellowing "MAIL CAWL".. Got a beeg package full of paper & rags and a few other things—It is very fine for <u>one</u> soltger—but do momma realize I gotta offer stuff to fifty or more? How can I give away one raisen to each? Everything in box will come in handy to <u>me</u>— tho .. Fourth platoon man came in—Everyone screams—"Watch your stuff—nail everything down" etc

December 21

Fear Drosh—

Just now I'm up on the front line or outpost—right over there where I'm pointing are the Germans—They can be heard talking and walking at night— I'm on a telephone—and have to try to wake someone on the other end to report—Last night someone asked "Who's doing that whistling?"—It was none other than Fanset—who I thought was far away with another outfit— Not too much noise except when patrols go out and call for artillary—Sitting outside my dug-out now with a steel helmet on—just in case—

Goobye

*Sodium hydroxide—a reference to his college chemistry experiments.

December 23

Dear PawPaw

Been a walking day—Tramped thru villages this morning—Came back—
Heard General Eisenhower's Order of the Day—Fell out—Played football—
Practiced for beeg parade which will take place tomorrow—Awarding of
honorary medals—We now have a Christmas tree in here trimmed with
greeting cards toilet tissue and inflated rubbers—Finally won a game of
checkers—By that time it was late for chow—But I managed to get some
peaches & bread—Leaving shortly for "The Song of Bernadette"

December 24

Dear NaOH—

The day is over as far as work goes—My checker board is in popular demand
—To date I have the fine average of one win and twenty-two losses! I am
waiting for a can of water & socks to heat up on the stove so I can wash 'em—
It is cold with a snap out—and clear—We stood before our barracks this
morning listening to our big band jumble over "Serenade for Strings" "Donkey
Serenade" and "White Christmas," latter number choked with sound of our
marching feet—We clumped over frozen mud to a remote but vast "Parade"
ground—waited with running noses while purple hearts and other awards
were presented an ear-straining distance away—Tank rumbled behind us, its
white star drawing our eyes—"Could be German," I ventured—"watch it
spray the whole batallion when it reaches cover"—They laughed and stamped
their feet—watched a French nurse and her shiny red car—Heard hoarse
commands—began to strut and squint in the sunlight—Saw light rippling on
swinging arms—flashing on rifles—Felt the breeze against our legs—hustled
in haste (how else can you?) to our bee-hive of a barrack—

  Beautiful Christmas tree over in the corner—full of greeting cards, inflated
rubbers and stringy toilet paper strands—Tonight it should be fairly joyous
especially if champagne is brought from town—Just returned from a sandbag
orientation of a village—Everyone is heading away from a taut rubber, which
is bulging ominously from Sgt Kulka's mighty blasts—As I write you are home
—Tell me 'bout it—In our mess hall is prominently printed (in German): "A
maiden and a glass of wine—These cure all needs. And he who doesnt drink
or kiss is as good as dead"—

~ CHRISTMAS ~

1944

Dear Peeple:

A year ago today I wrote you a letter sitting in my cluttered Benning hut—
silent but mighty meaningful—as Christmas wrappings, trimmings and boxes
reposed on the floor, beds and footlockers. I remember Dick Gist on the edge
of his bed—holding his obviously clogged head—It was kinda cold in there
even tho the stove was hissing. And quiet—except for that—as all the guys
hadn't as yet staggered in from chow. The light wasn't coming in too well—yet
outside the frost was fuming in the sun—I thought of Aunty Tobie's cookies—
still in my barrack bag and knew they'd have to be eaten before the next
morning—when we'd start our tedious trek to the range—

Today it's not too different—well maybe—I don't mean that exactly
—I woke up this morning; saw the glazed glittering windows, the empty
champagne bottles on the table beside my empty checker board, the motionless
lumps of sleeping bags, the reddish light glaring at our simpering Christmas
tree, an urchin in fine clothing—a Cinderella before the fireplace.—Reminders
of the night before, a pleasant night, sober and insane—snaggle-toothed
Taylor indignantly struggling in the soothing arms of Hadleberg—forced to
hear of former Christmas eve delicacies; Hadleberg, a poem, and thoughts of
the future; the cautious sips of red wine and later champagne—"cess-pool
7-Up";—vicious but victorious games of checkers—my first lucky streak;
Kamins and Murlin and houses of France and England and California;
midnight—"Merry Christmas"; red faces smiling in from midnight mass;
Boomer and Walters and Reimers and a dictionery and a list of words; sleep—

They sing now, filled with beer and too much food. They sing—with their
arms locked around their necks, and the tune runs along—around this table—
out the door with the draft—we are very fortunate—it is almost too good to
be true—"control yourself"—the captain told us. "This is the opportune time
for the enemy to strike" and we ran in, felt the heat of the stove, glanced at our
bed to be sure we had 128 rounds of ammunition and the hand grenades—

I took a picture of them eating; saw the empty smeared mess kit—felt
the turkey, mashed potatoes, sweet potatoes, asparagus, dressing, bread,
cranberry sauce, chocolate butterscotch pudding, three-layer cake, bitter
taste of beer, wondered.

I am fairly clean—the gum I chew so hard is comforting. Olive drab moves about me—I am thinking of all of you now—there <u>are</u> good men—They are here—"At home," the captain told us . . "—your next Christmas dinner—at home"—

McIntyre was standing up, smirking at a turkey leg—Boomer swayed in unison with the meaty limb—"At <u>eash</u>," he bellowed, "The next appearance will be 1st Sgt. Silber, better known as 'Blister Bag'—who will act as Santy Klash"—Deep silence. McIntyre choked on his turkey. Tears seeped steadily— "Mother always told me there weren't no Santy Claus," he wailed—

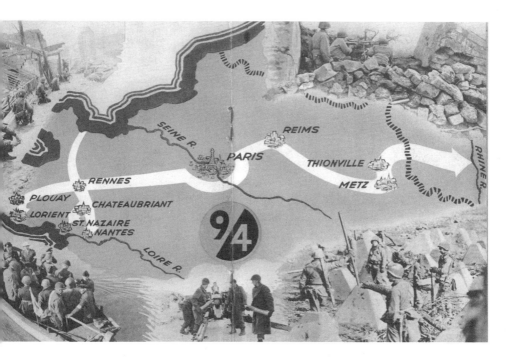

September 1944 to March 1945. From Brittany, the 94th Infantry Division traveled in boxcars to the German winter and the Rhine. *Lower right,* dragon's teeth on the Siegfried Line. "Passed by Censor for mailing home." From "On the Way—the Story of the 94th Infantry Division," Information and Education Division, ETOUSA (European Theater of Operations, U.S. Army).

Only hours to go

FRANCE

Once more it is hello:

But for me it is goodbye. The holiday ends tonight—I shall sleep in underwear on a bed before a stove under lights that work—Tomorrow night I will be far away, stepping closer in the new adventure that is in store for us—I have worn clean clothing—eaten well—seen movies—played—worked—relaxed— These have been days to remember—Discussions—talks—fights—singing— checkers—reading—writing—showers. Today we roared away in chill, bright air—roared over steaming frosty roads—Ran a problem with smoke and noise—

Showered today—washed and dried some clothes—it's the same old evening—with talk and whistling and poker games and guys writing— Survived a mad scramble to see "Louisiana Hayride" and "Girl Crazy" last nite—Judy Canova had us sobbing on each other's shoulders with disgust— Judy Garland had us sighing—and expectant for her tickling presence —Going back we watched our breaths—talked of blizzards in Minnesota and Dakota—

So tomorrow we will shiver on the trucks—cigarettes will glow—diffusing with the rising sun—and we'll look for towns and the women there to wave to . . and later on we'll stop and get adjusted—things will seem so natural— They always do—

John W. "Jack" Fanset *(right)*, who was killed in Butzdorf, Germany, and M.D. at Fort Benning, Georgia

Sidney R. Ellicott in Oakland, California

ASTP at Fort Benning (one-third of photo shown). I am at the far left, in the third row from the top.

M.D. ("Sunny"), 1944

My brother Burr, 1943

With Mother while on furlough,
May 1944. The "Big House" is
behind us.

With Father while on furlough, May 1944.

My third platoon—while I was on furlough. *In front,* Master Sergeant (later Lieutenant) "Boomer" Flynn. *First row,* my squad *(left to right):* S-Sgt Kovac, Pfc Tipton, Pfc Springsteen, Pfc Costello, Pvt Bryson, Pvt Fast Horse, Pfc Brown—Shorty Jones (2nd squad). *Third row, far right,* Sergeant Kulka, my squad leader.

In Nantes, France. *On reverse:* "My pockets are bulging with souvenirs."

In reserve at Lorient, France. *Front,* "Yogi" Reimers. *Rear, left to right:* Tom Costello, Tom Walters (killed in Butzdorf), Bob Murlin, Dorman Brown.

In my white jacket, Brittany woods.

The prisoners' "cage," Barentin, France.

Archibald "Mac" McKendry at the chateau in Barentin.

The 94th in Paris, September 1945. M.D. is top row center.

Caricature of M.D.,
Folies Bergère, Paris.

With Arthur
Bullman, Paris.

At Camp
Lucky Strike.

Soldiers boarding
the *Enterprise*,
December 1945.

Portrait of M.D., 2002. Photo by Philip James Herman.

3

Blood and Snow:
Germany, January 1945

"Why am I alive" I say over and over "Why am I alive"

January 8, 1945

GERMANY

Dear Patient Parents (maybe)

At the moment I'm in a dark upstairs room of a German home—My squad sits in shadow on beds and near a stove. We are fairly cozy in here—shut sufficiently away from a frigid snow storm which whirls outside and howls thru one large gap and many bullet holes in the side of the house— . . Being GIs—we naturally had one thought—before thawing our feet and getting settled—namely: souveniers—what a collection—the people left in a rush— evidently leaving photographs—identification and ration books—pictures —money—jewelry—rare rocks—furniture—toys—food—and books! millions of 'em—found a huge red book entitled "Adolf Hitler"—tore him out and now have him for a pin up boy—

—VIBRATIONS—

We had the well known 40 and 8 cars—we had 22 men in our small rambling crate—we could look out the side or sit in the straw on the floor and read or play cards—under the straw there were slats between the boards. We could tell the way the wind rushed thru—our bulky packs and equipment were hung on nails above us—the day passed quickly as we watched the country change and whiten under snow—or we could lean out over the 2×4 crossing our doorway and yell to other guys on other cars—either the train barely crept or else it simply jerked—wherever we'd stop you'd see the guys bounding across the tracks to squat behind the freights—Once we stopped long enough to find a small stove and fuel—Frenchmen would stoop quickly to grab our butts and discarded rations—some guys got it into their heads to attach strings to the cigarettes and jerk them away .. Night was the only real problem—there simply was no room—but we scrambled together in grotesque heaps laying on legs and boxes—the last nite a train-load of WACs passed but two feet from us—A cramped ride in truck delivered me to this spot—where I wish you good nite from Germany

January 10

Dear NaOH:

My first night in Deutschland was warm and comfortable—unfortunately not a blueprint for the future—Yesterday we moved in and took over the mess of a once beautiful village—It didnt even look as if the people had paused to dress in their hectic flight. Since I said that 24 hrs have passed—We are occupying a lovely suite in the town hall— .. the living accommodations came quite as a shock—we could hardly have been more miserable than we were en route— We all had the box-car blues—the color of our frozen limbs—22 men rode in our car—a rattling—bumping—filthy—drafty nightmare—and yet looking back we did have some fun—gazing at the scenery—yelling at other cars— But at night it wasnt too delightful wondering when your feet would crack off or the packs hung above you would fall—During stops we'd have hot coffee and "C" rations—fires would spring up fed by pilfered coal and wood— Frenchmen would slouch up and down alert for cigarette butts and rations which they'd scoop up with zeal—before long they became easy victims of G.I. pranks—butts jerked out of grasping fingers by slight pressure on attached but concealed strings—At last the ordeal ended—Now I look out, see the crack and black puffs of shells, feel the windows rattle—

II

Couple Sundays ago I went to Nantes again— .. the whore house district is reached by climbing a winding sidewalk past crumbling ruins—We finally selected No 4—Over in a corner scrunched up a midget thing sat slurping soup—Brown and I sat down and began to read papers—barbershop style—

now and then two girls shivering near a stove would leap into a dance making sure no one present would have to crane their necks to see what they wanted to see—At times the door would open to erupt a flushed and hazy young man followed by a sly smile in doll clothes—a third member of our party finally selected a blonde and departed—Brown and I are peacefully reading papers—One red headed wench whirls about stretching tight her garments to assure the customer that a volcano is underneath—we do not mind as long as we are unmolested—but suddenly they start coming over—and lean across the table dangling things—they glide their fingers over my face and shoulders and one in particular aint bad looking—but soch manners—I have to put my helmet over an appropriate spot to provide protection—after assuring them that I am penniless and sexless they depart—with the only English words they know—not necessarily printable—It is New Years eve—we buy expensive champagne for the boys and head back—Lil Morton has rid again—

January 13, 1945

GERMANY

Mine Dyar Peeple—

This letter is wropped in with my stuff. I hope you never get it—Tomorrow at dawn we drive off into our first attack—Somebody may be hurt—All the guys I've lived with so many months are here in the room—talking loud—playing —"sinkum"—cleaning their rifles—noone is really very calm—we just have another big problem tomorrow—only someone will be shooting back—the Sergeant came in the room with the sun a while ago—told us very simply—funny feeling running up and down my back—no doubt you've received my letters—And know how pleasant these last few days have been—even got your mail!—Good to hear and visualize goings on at home in such a homey setting. I hope things will carry on as usual—no matter what—maybe the war will end sometime and you can really be happy again—good luck Burr—love to Mom & Dad

Mort

There was reason enough for this farewell letter. The "Bulge" had been stabilized in the north by the end of December, and the drive into Germany could be resumed. Our 94th Division, now part of General Patton's Third Army, was ordered to make the first crack in the Siegfried "Switch" line, which guarded communications centers in the Saar-Moselle rivers area. It was one of

the coldest and snowiest winters on record, but that was not to be our main problem. Ahead of us were "pillboxes, bunkers, anti-tank ditches, mine fields, zeroed-in forests and dragon's teeth." I did not know that then, or the letter might have been more somber.

[January 22, 1945]

"IT"

The Sergeant came in with the sun that morning, but chilled us to the bone. "We attack at dawn," he said. We shudder slightly and feel internal tension, just as if he's asked us to pull K.P. We were sitting around a table, talking, playing "Sinkum." Everybody talks, laughs, shakes, smirks. Gradually it all wears off like the coating of a Chiclet, with something left to chew on.

Methodically we clean and oil every bullet, every centimeter of our rifles. The work was slow and tedious, and we didn't talk much then—just glanced up once in a while to watch the snow and bleakness of the hills outside. Artillary shook the windows occasionally, but we'd become accustomed to it already. Our suite was warm and comfortable, and the noon meal tasted all right. I sat down and write a letter starting "I hope you never get this—". We relaxed, read, thought. The sergeant brought in maps with "Secret" scribbled all over. It was the plan of Tittengen [Tettingen], and our job was plainly marked in red, with a big x in the middle labled "Suicide corner." Very calmly we went over it—just another problem.

By nightfall our equipment was packed and ready. I dozed on my inner-spring mattress in semi-darkness, watching faces in the glow of cigarettes. The men were talking low—all young, intelligent. They spoke of home and the post-war world. . . naturally, not forced. . . . I wondered how many would see home again . . .

It was 2:00 A.M. We got up groggy; doused ourselves under layers of flour, ripped white curtains into strips to insert beneath our helmet netting. Flour was swirled about on the floor as we left with mournful glances and a swish of resignation. We looked ghostly on the silver road. Breakfast consisted of steak, fried potatoes and fruit salad. We bolted the food and slipped away to find our place in line. The column of men spiralled off, merging with the hills, vaguely suspended in gloomy greyness. It began to flow and ripple along. Devoid of a hampering pack, we glided smoothly. Fanset was beside me with two machine gun boxes. Walters was ahead. We laughed and joked like a boy and girl in a hayloft, knowing something was bound to happen. Fanset reminded me of

"The two Blue Gnus and a Yak" story I used to tell at Benning. It was crisp and our breaths were cloudy vapors in the frigid air . . .

We passed Borg and Wochern, the last outposts, the positions we'd dug and finally reached a rising slope of woods. The attack began promptly at 0700 hours . . . Bands of a rosey hue were streaking across the already paling sky, soon obscured as our smoke shells lobbed in. Then the din increased in tempo with the artillary and mortar barrage. We filed slowly through the woods, flattening when necessary. Fanset dashed ahead—the last time I was to see him.

The whole sky was a flaming, boiling mass, and we didn't bother yelling to each other—just mutely picked our way. The Engineers' trail stopped abruptly at a road, in which an empty German tank huddled like a dormant mammoth. A brilliant orange flash outlined the figures of the men ahead. We panted down beside the tank, I saw the medics jerking forward, hunching down. Sgt. Dye was dead . . Sgt. Dye is dead. It kept running through my mind. Now came a treacherous field, clogged with snow, approaching the formidable dragon's teeth, tank nemesis of the Siegfried Line. In one superhuman dash we plowed our way to a stone wall, and dropped in convulsive heaps. The shells seemed to be on top of us. One by one we slipped over a gash in the wall and filtered forward among the dragon teeth into a graveyard. The church above us was taking a pounding. I pressed my nose against some cold granite, and heard shouting, and exploding of grenades in the town. We slithered down a slope to pause breathless in a garage. A German rifle was on the floor. We didn't touch it. Suddenly we realized we'd crossed "Suicide Corner." A German and an American, both dying, were glaring at each other and moaning for a medic. The German mortars had the range, but Nazis came pouring out to surrender. They'd been enjoying breakfast, and were evidently quite surprised and alarmed over the prospect of an empty stomach. Andy Rothenback rounded a corner to come face to face with a leering kraut. Both fired at once, but Andy hit home.

We watched Reimers search some men, then fanned out to a trench, conveniently provided by the Germans. It ran up a hill to a pillbox and beyond. Our second platoon had taken the pillbox and were dispersed along the rise. The order went out to evacuate—the TDs were moving in to blow up the pillbox. We cowered by the church, watching the lumbersome things rumble up. Suddenly I see a green flash, hear a terrible roar, follow the heaving of the hull. "My God, it's hit!" I think. But it was only the effect of the 75. Four times it fires. Four times it misses. The Germans move back and nonchalantly set up their mortar. Soon the church is sagging like an idiot's jaw. I catch shrapnel on my hand and shoulder, and decide to vacate. Kettler and I dive into a trench shoulder deep with snow, and shovel frantically. Our perspiration wins, however. We are shortly standing in water, and the heat of our bodies has also melted the mud on the sides of the trench. It oozes down our legs. We're all cramped up, sweating between sneezes, feeling like a drunk on Sunday morning. Two bullet holes appear in a tree inches from my head. Snipers are indignantly spraying us from Butzdorf, a town farther down the valley. Dodging artillary, pudgy Sgt. Kovak races in with a scowling Nazi officer he found hiding in a ditch. Our battalion commander radios back: "Objective taken." McClune returns: "Fine, take the next town!"

Just like that: no plans, no nothing. Even though we took Tittengen in a mere thirty minutes we are a trifle winded. Soon we leave our positions and scramble down a road to assembly. The whip of bullets automatically increases the speed of our advance. At the center of town it gets slightly hot again, and we crowd back into the trench. Everyone crams himself together like a young embryo, and waits for the terrific pounding to cease. It doesn't. Sgt. Asp calmly shoots himself in the foot and joyfully limps away. I crawl along on hands and knees, pass machine gunners, stiff bodies. I put my hand down on a face, feel it crunch and gurgle, and experience a momentary nausea.

By degrees we work down to the edge of town. Our First Sgt. is already swinging his bulk around, cheering us no little. Guys go by with bloody smiles. A 200 yard stretch of potential death separates us from Butzdorf. The hill slopes up to the left and German positions. A rickity iron fence provides the only cover, although big black shell craters are rapidly mushrooming up in the snow. A brownish building, subsequently dubbed "Halfway House" stands solidly in the center of the clearing. We stream out steadily, following up the forward elements, which have already entered the town. We get caught out in the open; Jim Nance, dangling fingers, and Carl Floren, crouching over a demolished radio, wave us on. Lt. Dunville and Hinds gallop by, waving us back. Everyone wheezes in the snow. "Fgawdsake, make up your minds!" The gouging concussions of the nearby mortar blasts practically blow us into snowballs. We grope our way into craters, and lie there, choking, coughing up soot. Big John McCoy tosses out a dead Jerry. I peer over at Murlin's weary eyes. "Is this convenient?" I shout, "Is this a pretty affair?" We finally find our way into Butzdorf. Doorways are packed. The first sight that greets everyone is the Captain, lying in the road with not all of his head. He stares stupidly at us, feebly attempting to put his helmet back on. We later learn he lived as far as Cherbourg. Hinds' feet protrude from a doorway. A medic runs in. We all avoid a glossy, unexploded shell.

From somewhere someone is calling me. I find Sgt. Sanniec in a concrete stable. The town is being cleaned out. We gaze out the windows and set ourselves for the explosions. Kettler, Murlin, and I ease up against the wall, trying to absorb some sunlight. Our gloves sizzle on a ledge. Tom Costello quietly steps in. His face is expressionless, "Fanset is dead," he says.

Things calm down, but we expect the inevitable counter-attack. We relieve ourselves in a corner, and pry out our C rations. Sanniec comes in and we move. I see Walters, tell him Fanset is dead. He says he never thought Fanset would get killed. We're in a fairly decent house—only the upper story is battered. We're on the edge of town facing Halfway House, Tittengen and the pillbox. Our basement is full of hastily left kraut mess gear, a bedded shelf, and even a stove. Not too bad. Upstairs we designate a room with large broken windows and a slot at the head of the cellar stairs as guard posts. The prolonged lull is irritating, as we find ourselves freezing. We realize our field jackets are not exactly adequate in drafty places. Big anti-tank rockets are scattered about upstairs. "They're not heavy," says Kettler. "I picked one up!"

A heavy machine gun crew joins us and we help them erect barricades. As we settle down for the night, Kettler gets a bright idea to slip open a feather mattress and crawl in for warmth. Before long the place is infested with feathers. For five days, we sleep, eat and breathe feathers! Patrols are already out. A waxed, crumbling old loaf of bread is our supper.

About three in the morning I am knocking my shanks on the wall upstairs. I almost turn inside out as a horrible moaning wail shrieks down across the fields like a million banshees on a rampage. The night is immediately split with sharp criss-crossing lights. It is the belated counter attack. The burp guns rattle and cough—our machine guns answer from Tittengen. Hoarse shouting forms a mighty background for the furious action. Spent bullets zoom in all directions, stinging our eyes with their dazzling trail. All of us are nervously expecting the worst, but the main body of enemy troops sweep down from the woods to our right, and never reach our side of town. Meanwhile Sanniec, McCoy, Murlin, and Brown are "mowing 'em down." German medics take up abandoned guns, and beaucoups of wounded jerries are crawling all over the place—moaning and heil hitlering. We later learn that four companies have attacked us at the point of a gun, after a fifteen mile hike in full field and overcoats. It is a slaughter. By morning 900 German bodies blotch the snow.

Birds flit out of the haze and twitter lifelessly on shredded limbs. The sun is a sickly red behind a sheen of snowflakes, which drift slowly down to veil the bodies and melt with little hisses on clotting blood . . .

We act like we're drugged. The smoke, dust and plaster clog the creases of our clothing. We stand around like fools, then slide into a timeless wandering, with a reasonable amount of peace. Supplies are carried from Tittengen. Three nights drag by. Our first "meal" was a cold meatball so filled with garlic that most of them found a snowy grave. The Germans had uncanny accuracy with their mortar. We had a water hole twenty feet from the house. Three yanks and a disemboweled cow grew rigid at its edge. For some reason I made my many trips safely, dipping in my German pail with a plop, and running back. One big surprise was the arrival of mail and the remarkable ten in one rations. In the latter were paper towels and soap, and appreciatively we washed.

The fifth night patrols reported enemy movements. It was my turn to work with the carrying party. Over at the CP we whispered in darkened halls, slipped out shortly with empty jerricans. With maddening ease we'd work our way to Tittengen, freezing time and again as flares lit up the sky. Somehow I managed two trips with the cruel weight of water cans and anti-tank mines. Bodies were being taken across that night too. Fanset started his last journey. After ten in one rations, blankets, sleeping bags, and mail had been delivered to the CP, I was relieved. A voice revealed that the second battalion was attacking the pillbox at dawn. Back at the house I snuggled down in the filth and feathers and slept.

When I went on guard I put a can of pork and apple loaf in the oven to warm. By 0700 the light was growing and the wump, wump, wump of mortars and whine of shells brought in the morning with a rush. It didn't take us long to figure out that we were attacked, not attacking. This time the Heinies really meant business. We blinked as a grinding stream of white tanks churned in front of us. Little helmeted heads were bobbing and the black cross on the side grew larger. We were playing host to the rejuvenated 11th Panzer Division. Our artillary was viciously tearing up the surroundings but the tanks didn't falter. Six of the monsters push up to the Halfway House and stop, thus accomplishing two purposes: they have a shield and have completely cut us off from the "mainland." We are the thumb in the anthill. Poor Andy, we think.

The boys on the other side of town are just as amazed as we are. Wylie has his pants down and is straining in a corner. The shout of enemy tanks sends him scurrying across the floor, trailing trousers in a cloud of dust. He procures his bazooka, finds a target, makes one good shot, and returns to resume his other exursions. W.C. Pillow jams a tank turret with his machine gun, stops it with his bazooka, charges out with a beehive, blows it up, takes up his machine gun again to riddle the occupants; Kamins is wild with excitement, as his rocket shatters a tread. Even in the Halfway House, the men are far from mortified with fear. They keep poking their heads out every so often to bang away at the tanks and systematically plug Germans on the field. Hundreds of the creatures are floundering about in extreme agony. Those who survive artillary blasts are demanding our capitulations. "Surrender Johny Jerkoff— you are surrounded!" they scream.

Our house is being knocked to pieces but it still provides some protection. A piece of shrapnel splits my kneecap, but I soon forget about it as other little matters keep asserting themselves. For some strange reason the tanks swerve about and bump away. The quiet is baffling. Boomer Flynn crashes in to tell us we've beaten them off. . . . nothing more to fear . . . reinforcements on the way. It is almost noon. Jim McLees appears in the shadows, a hole through the front and back of his helmet, a drooping scarlet bandage over his right ear. The bullet had swerved around the rim of his helmet, shearing off his ear, coming out the front. Jim is slightly dazed. He wants to go after a sniper in the woodpile, but we hold him back. Doc Spicer, bloody to the elbows, comes around. All our officers are cringing in the CP cellar. The first Sgt. is running the company, bellowing out orders, cursing at the unreliable walkie-talkies. He announces that someone is to run out to Halfway House with bazooka ammo. Tom Costello and Ray Collins scamper out—ludicrous under stacks of rockets. Walt Taylor has made another of these heart-in-mouth excursions to Tittengen to demand more bazookas from the colonel. He gets them.

All this is done just in time, for word is with us that tanks and infantry are sighted over yonder hill. This is the crusher, no mere reconnaisance. The din is indescribable. The impertinent tanks follow the same old course, ganging up on Halfway House, rupturing our connections with civilization. We feel worse than uneasy. Before our last radio goes on the blink, it feebly expounds that we've officially been given up by the regiment—we're to hold out to the bitter end . . . the country will never forget our valiant efforts . . . bla, bla, bla . . . We practically blow up, more over the words than the seriousness of the situation. Although we are unaware of it, the infantry is cautiously moving behind a wave of tanks, 33 altogether. Before long our total of kills mounts to 15. The colonel is having his difficulties at Tittengen. He drags out the tank destroyer commander, shows him some clearly defined targets. The captain shakes his head, he can't see a thing. The colonel is incredulous. He orders, he begs, he pleads, but the tank destroyers refuse to budge or expose themselves in any way, claiming they don't have a clear lane of fire. All vehicles bringing up anti-tank guns are thoroughly pulverized by the pillbox crew. The Germans abandon caution and make the final dash.

Walters is popping away at the heads. I tell him don't, we'll only draw direct 88 fire. I was right. The room was quivering. Our ears were ringing. Our chests were throbbing. We shook like wet washing—a cold, creepy uncontrollable shaking. Only our minds remained clear. The rubble was piling high in the center of the room. . . . our ceiling was ready to bury us beneath it. Solemnly we discussed our procedure when the Germans, expected momentarily, entered the house. "Walters," I say, "it seems we are in a position not particularly desirable to our state of welfare. Our careers are jeopardized. I strongly urge that we prepare for the worst." We agree to hide in wine barrels, hoping for an eventual American victory. Someone is pounding on the wall. Chandler is hit . . . a slug caught him in the head . . he plunged head first down the cellar stairs. . . . Walter's eyes are big and brown and expectant. For the first time in our lives we know the feeling of utter hopelessness, the dread sensation of approaching doom. The turmoil within us almost gives way, but we are listening for our artillary. When it comes, it is right on top of us. Luckily the patterns had been drawn in on us, keeping the Germans at a reasonable distance. This factor alone, saved us.

Walters has his hands in his pockets, looking out the window. A shell bursts outside the window to my right rear. Shrapnel wirrs across the room, cuts through Tom like a sewing needle, slicing a path from head to stomach. He explodes apart in a torrent of blood. "Get out the door!" I shout. With his hands still in his pockets, he turns halfway, starts to jerk forward, choking, gasping, sputtering, then settles face down to the floor, gurgling away his life. At the head of the stairs I collapse in a pool of Chandler's blood, tell them Walters is hit. Kettler and Doc take off and return with something still. Jenkins and I force our eyes away. We know Walters is dead.

We give up our guard posts altogether, leave one man atop the stairs, and slump down in the basement. Chandler is groaning. Boomer is shaken to tears at the sight of Tom. He tells us to pull out. The machine gunners had long ago departed. We're to try to reach Tittengen under smoke. At the door Chandler breaks down: "I can't make it." "You've got to try." One by one we make our suicide dashes, passing pleading men. I sail through a doorway of beckoning hands ahead of a whistling 88. Now that we're gathered in this place and the cp next door, the Germans can concentrate their fire. They do. Men keep toppling over my shoulders. I struggle up for air. A wild-eyed kid holds up his hand. "Look, my thumb's blown off!" The ragged stump is maroon like our basement floor at home. We're all bunched up on a stairway. Guys are lying on the floor and propped in corners. I look around . . . what is going on? I see the drawn, bearded faces, torn clothes, staring eyes, yards of dirty bandages. Men are muttering, babbling. No, I decide, it isn't possible. The shell-shocked stand up and look at us. "Can't you see I'm bleeding?" they whimper. No one answers. . . .

We finally crowd into a tiny room beneath some stairs . . . still the men on the outside keep getting hit. For four hours we stand shoulder to shoulder, softly talking, sweating, shaking. The smoke had failed us—lifted before it hit the ground. We're to try to make a run for freedom when it gets dark. Meanwhile we're ordered to return to our positions. Some men go back, find Germans, kill them, rip open ten in one boxes, urinate on the food, return to us. Others go after the wounded. Sgt. Flynn lugs in a box of ten in ones. Courteously we divide up the cold food and pass it around. From a can of corn I get needed water.

In the CP the lights are out. Everyone is sprawled in the corridors. The 1st Sgt. stuffs his pockets full of mail, burns the rest. Our blankets, sleeping bags, and overcoats lie untouched against the walls. Rothenbach has one of two working radios. He hails us from Halfway House. Sgt. Smith croaks half hysterically into the mouthpiece. "Just checkin'" cracks unperturbed Andy.

We look out. The tanks are brown shadows lined up before us. Other tanks cover all the street intersections. Everyone is still determined to make a run for it. We improvise stretchers out of ladders, and men are selected to carry back the wounded. Only about forty of us are left. The confusion mounts as squads are assembled in makeshift fashion in the dark, and groups of six are counted off. McIntyre gazes up into the countenance of one number six man, finds it is a kraut, loaded to capacity with grenades. Close examination reveals a large number of Germans who have been arrogantly strolling in our midst, intending to surrender. We take them along. Outside it is a frightening orange and amber, dim and foreboding, with a fury of sleet and a howling wind thrown in for good measure. Groups of six are on their way, lost in the swirling mist. Little Tom Costello lingers by Halfway House, not knowing whether he's seeing Germans, or if he'll be mistaken for one. He compares it to a Bela Lugosi thriller. Those still alive at Halfway House will leave when our last group goes by. I start out fifth but break the tape a close second. The musty blackness of the nearest Tittengen house releases all our fears in a wave of relief, even though the danger is far from past. Oddly enough, not a shot was fired at us. It was just our night, evidently, for 48 hours later Company A,

302 was to go through the same ordeal and emerge with only five men and the topkick. Our Battalion had already pulled out. In the Co. F CP we stumbled about bumping into our men and Nazis. At last someone came to lead us out, and we staggered away into the bitter cold, stormy night. I glimpsed Kettler rubbing out a cigarette. M'gawd, the thought struck me, he'd never smoked before!

We trailed out past the dragon teeth, through the woods, and followed a winding road to Wochern. Every few feet we fell down from weariness. The storm was having its grisly fun, pitching us on like sacks of potatoes. Wochern swayed forelornly. We were so dazed we didn't notice the sleet had turned to biting, soaking rain. But hot coffee and a blanket were waiting for us. They led us gently like pampered goats. I felt my beard. It was long and sticky, and my face and neck were burning with a rash. Why am I alive, I wondered. Why am I alive?

finis

This "IT" is from a version I rewrote (typed) in 1945. The original—lost with my belongings and eventually returned—was hand printed on both sides of extremely thin German paper through which the ink bled, so that the first twelve of seventeen pages cannot be transcribed.

ALSACE-LORRAINE

January 22, 1945

[from "IT"—original letter]
We are practically staggered as the unmistakable grinding rumble of tanks hits our ears—On they come—Above the racket we hear "Sieg Heil Sieg Heil Sieg Heil Sieg Heil" sounding like Santa Claus driving his reindeer in a blizzard—They don't stop but several of 'em all gang up on "Halfway House"—"Poor Andy," we whimper. "He is doomed." Meantime artillary is coming from all directions—we look like jack-in-the-boxes—Across town to our left Wylie is squatting—contentedly emptying his stomach—A tank looms into view—Wylie wobbles forward dragging his pants along the floor dangling something; shortly loads bazooka—W.T. Pillow is ducking fire—shooting his machine gun—picks up a bazooka—stops a tank—grabs a beehive—dashes out—blows up the tank—returns; pops off retreating crew—"Where is the T.D.'s," we wonder—In the halfway house they wonder too—soberly glare down the barrel of an 88—decide against carving their

initials on it—The tankers are wheeling about—sieging and heiling—I see lot
of 'em get popped off by Taylor and DiPaula and Regalis who shot one by
firing thru a tree—Walters is beside me blazing away—we finally stop him—
convinced that we'll draw point-blank fire by the tank—which we get anyway
—I watch the walls slide slowly apart—for some strange reason the tanks
retreat—Unknown to us many are getting destroyed. Next to us at the head
of the cellar stairs Jenkins calls for assistance—Chandler is slumped down—
hit in the head—as tankers sprayed the windows—Somehow Boomer and
Doc reach us—We learn the machine gun crew has a radio—but it is soon
knocked out—The action is narrowed down to artillary bombardment—we
sit—silent in the basement—I am shaking all over—everybody is—yet our
thoughts are calm—Boomer reassures us—and we wait—knowing the attack
isn't over—we force ourselves to eat—realizing it is the thing to do—At
Halfway House they are prespiring rather rapidly—Taylor streaks thru the
hail of fire and procures a bazooka—Costello and Collins gallop out with
ammunition—The tanks return—we figure it is all over—Tanks and infantry
sighted we hear—Walters and I are alone in a corner room—we plan what to
do—in case we are hit—We know we are lost—decide to crawl away and hide
in a cider barrel after the Germans enter the house—The terrible feeling of
utter hopelessness is recorded in my mind for the first time—but we are
calm—just the slow cold shutters crawl upon us—Again the tanks pass us up
for "Halfway House"—one gets blown up on a mine—two others suddenly
stop—but we think they'll come rattling up the streets any minute—not to
mention enemy infantry—at 1430 the regiment officially gives us up as lost—
The order to evacuate comes later—but the smoke lifts and we see this is
suicide—a shell lands outside the window—opposite me on the left of the
room Walters stands with his hands in pockets—I see shrapnel plunge across
his face and neck—blood come pouring out in solid sheets of crimson—I
stare stupified as he wobbled forward falls flat gurgling—I find myself all
folded up on the cellar stares—he is so white—so white—

My head hurts—Chandler is moaning—some of us sit in the dark
basement—I hate to use the flashlight—it is so sticky—I look at my pants—
not long tho—Boomer and McLees appear—McLees has a bloody patch
down half his face—a hole is in the exact center of his helmet—some miracle
has swerved the bullet—it only took off a piece of his ear—Mac's eyes are
glazed—he wants to crawl out the window after a sniper in a woodpile but we
don't let him—All over individual actions are going on—We don't know
about—McCoy blasts his way into the C.P.—We find our machine gunners
have left—Kettler drops his cigarette. I blinked—knowing he'd never smoked

before—"I'm taking up a bad habit," he smiles at Spicer—So we leave—
Chandler gets up—cracks at the door—"I'll never make it"—"You gotta
try"—Chandler—we say—trying to mask our fear—So we successfully
navigate to another building next to the c.p.—we escape the mortars—but
others don't—They're dragged in—and tired bloody Spicer goes to work—
We're all huddled in a corner—hearing white flag talk—hearing stories of
other groups—how Tsgt Mcintyre found a German nonchalantly bringing up
the rear of one of our columns—of German prisoners giving up—being shot
at by their own men to prevent capture—stories of bravery and horror—I
look around at the haggard bearded faces—some quite bloody—Boomer
dashes out and returns with a case of 10 in 1's We divide it up and eat
silently—A shell explodes outside the door—somebody falls over me—
"Look," he says my thumb is blown off—it wasn't bleeding—just a raw
stump—the color of our basement floor at home—we move the wounded to
another room and crowd in—Men are braving runs back and forth from the
c.p.—It is definite we are to move out under cover of darkness—We're all on
edge—but I hear plenty of snickering with the shocked whispers—most of
us are shell-shocked—we're all fatigued beyond imagination—We wait—
breathing heavily as darkness comes on—and cold and sleet—In the c.p.
a German captive views proceedings with amusement—It is necessary to
destroy radios and identifications—I think of sleeping bags and blankets
piled over there—The first sergeant is gallently running the whole show—
bubbling over with efficiency—This dawns on everybody—They realize he
is holding them together—

The confusion is maddening—but finally men are assigned to stretchers
improvised for the wounded—At last I move off—in a group led by Flynn—
We waste—no time—streaking across the snow—ghostly forms in the
halflight—sleet beating against us—wind howling—Again I wonder "Why
don't they shoot?" Costello is standing by Halfway House—scared to the
gills—thinking he'd be shot for a Nazi—The atmosphere is that of a Lugosi
thriller—Then we hover in darkness—get led away over treacherous hills to
a night of uneasy sleep—We are so filthy—so unbelieving—but the torture is
dropping behind us—the tension is slackening—"Why am I alive" I say over
and over "Why am I alive"—

Mort

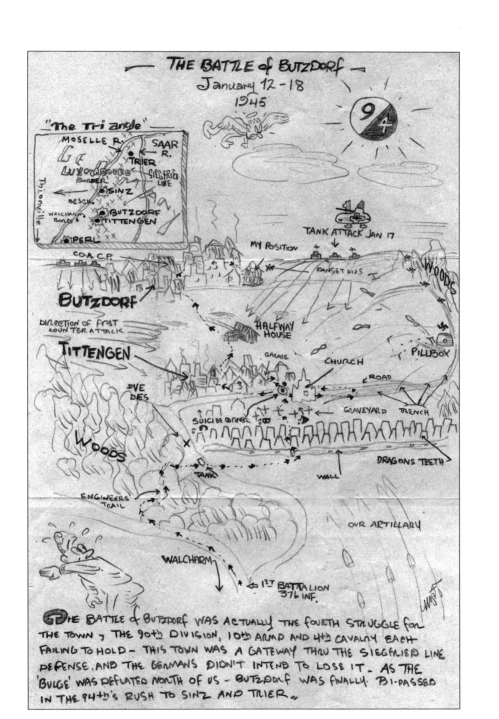

THE BATTLE of BUTZDORF
January 12-18
1945

94

"The Tri angle"

MOSELLE R.   SAAR R.
Gε   TRIER   SIEGFRIED LINE
LUXOMBOURG
Border
← SINZ   BESCH.
WALCHARM   BUTZDORF
BORG   TITTENGEN
PERL

Thionville

TANK ATTACK JAN 17

MY POSITION
FANSET DIES   WOODS

CO A C.P.

BUTZDORF

DIRECTION OF FIRST COUNTER ATTACK

HALFWAY HOUSE

TITTENGEN

GARAGE   CHURCH   PILLBOX

DVE DES   ROAD

WOODS   SUICIDE CORNER   GRAVEYARD   TRENCH

TANK   WALL   DRAGONS TEETH

ENGINEERS TRAIL   OUR ARTILLARY

WALCHARM   ← 1ST BATTALION 376 INF.

THE BATTLE of BUTZDORF WAS ACTUALLY THE FOURTH STRUGGLE FOR
THE TOWN, THE 90th DIVISION, 10th ARMD AND 4th CAVALRY EACH
FAILING TO HOLD - THIS TOWN WAS A GATEWAY THRU THE SIEGFRIED LINE
DEFENSE, AND THE GERMANS DIDN'T INTEND TO LOSE IT - AS THE
'BULGE' WAS DEFLATED NORTH OF US - BUTZDORF WAS FINALLY BI-PASSED
IN THE 94th's RUSH TO SINZ AND TRIER.

January 22

FRANCE

Gneetz?

A few days ago I was experiencing a new feeling—utter despair—Last night I sweated here over a detailed account of our last little escapade ["IT"]—I was strongly urged to read it—and did groggily—naturally the poor things thought it was so good—ought to be in "Yank"! etc etc—tomorrow I get the morning off to polish it for mimeographing—you'll get the horrific account in two wks—mama and papa wont! Somebody figured we'd been in combat so now I get another 5 bucks for the new (combat infantry man) badge—I've been vainly trying to straighten out my mess of an ammo bag—I have all your letters of the last 13 months! to read I have "Life," "Times," "Newsweeks"—I'd ask you for the pony New Yorker—only I know I'd never find the time to read it—At the moment we are sleeping in the back room on straw—Easy to see in these houses the methodical planning of the fiend Hitler—every village is a cog in the chain of fortresses—every house a pillbox complete with embrasures . . Oh there is so much to do—letters to write—stuff I wanna read—my fingers and thoughts are flying—Gad what a life—COME ON RUSSIA!—

Goombye

[undated]

Dear Padre:

Glad to hear you've finally finished the toll of inventory—Now you as I must take a bit of a rest—Houses around here are remarkable—they are all constructed for warfare—now more than ever we realize how long ago this was planned and developed—every village has a direct purpose in Hitler's plans—most are situated in such a way that they are well covered on flanks by other villages—an amazing system of fortresses—disguized under the open simplicity of the civilians

I've been intending to bring my adventures up to date—after our stay in England we embarked and landed on one of the invasion beaches—worked our way down to the St Lazaire Lorient area—The big city where I had a shower in a German barrack was Rennes . . I travelled practically the entire territory—know it even better than most of Minnesota—We lived in holes we dug—and hated the mud and rain—rest areas were nice later on—as we

stayed in barracks the Germans had used—When we collaborated with the
Free French I picked up most of the French I know . . Patrols went out—night
on guard is but a dream now—The box cars took us to the land of snow—the
hedgerows tapered away to fields and hills—the homes and people a far cry
from the meticulous Germans a few miles away

**The few days were hardly enough to rally ourselves and insufficient time for
replacements to arrive. Nevertheless we moved out on the twenty-fifth with two
other regiments, attempting once again to break through the "Switch" "so that
armor could pour through and clear out the Saar-Moselle triangle." Extra heavy
clothing and hoods protected us against the cold, but we had continuous deadly
exposure to Schu-mines and artillery on the road past Tettingen and Butzdorf
to Sinz.**

[undated]

The first story of Sinz (sent to Burr) will be sufficient—until I get up enough
energy to relate the entire thing again—However—there seems to be a
conflict of opinion on the actual "wounding incident"—this is the official
version:

Nearing 2000—the remaining members of our company were squatting in
muddy shell craters in the woods to the left of the Besch-Sinz road (see map)
—Some of us, including msef were gouging out chunks of mud to enlarge our
holes—word came down that we were being relieved by a battalion of the
302nd and soon they were groping their way toward us—My squad hastily
assembled by Sanniec's hole and we stumbled thru the snow and mud and
scorched stumps toward the road—The moon was coldly gleaming on dead
tanks and discarded weapons—By the time we reached the road—the rasping
seal-sound of 120 mortars was filling the air—and we plunged into a ditch on
the left of the road—A slight let-up came—other members of the squad were
calling around and so was I—a temporary lull had us scrambling down the
road—but into the snowy ditch we went again—McCoy was ahead of me—
Murlin was behind—I was facing Sinz (luckily) [heart side not exposed]—A
brilliant orange flash caught my eye northeast of me about 50 yards—and I
felt a burning in my upper arm—"I'm hit" I say (how original!)—The others
are going on—Murlin & Robt. Brew (of Chicago) are helping me to my feet
and are trying to get me to walk—but my side is caving in—and I'm sinking
back down on my stomach—I tell Murlin to go ahead—Brew stays with me—
gets a medic who goes back for a jeep—The shelling continues—guys keep

running by—The sky is aflame—I find it hard to breathe—my hood smothers me—my helmet rolls off at every concussion—a jeep rattles up—

By the by—we were in overcoats—Brew is ripping away the shoulder and is applying belt tourniquet to my arm—which is blooding no little—My rifle and belt are 20 yds ahead of me in the ditch—I aint the only wounded man around—they lie on the road on the edge of the woods—Our Red Cross jeep is overcrowded . .

The mortar fragment (actual size).

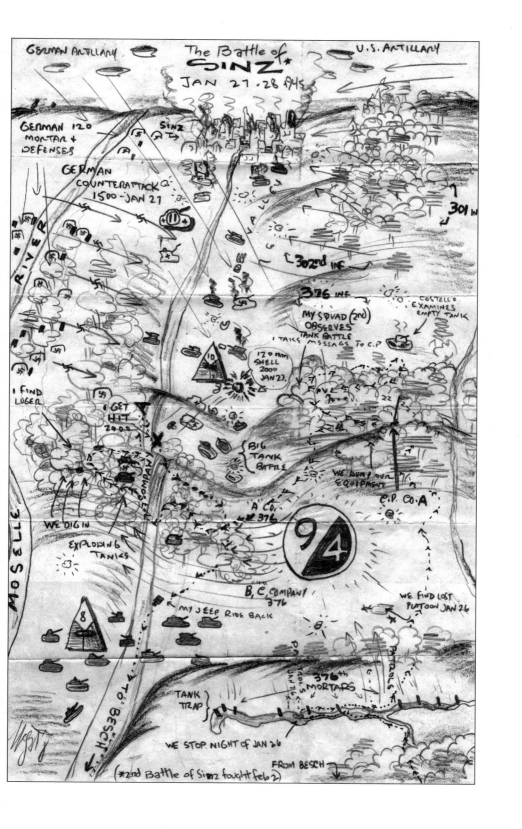

Early February 1945. From the hospital, back in England, I drew this in red
crayon on the reverse of the undated Sinz letter, p. 129.

4

The Recuperator: England,
February–June 1945

I can now breathe out of either lung as simply as opening or closing either eye!!

```
The filing time
(DMA17) 33 3 EXTRA GOVT WUX WASHINGTON DC VIA DULUTH MINN 10
MRS EVELEYN ELEVITCH=
     CARE MRS BLEHERT 1062 LINWOOD STPL=
REGRET TO INFORM YOU YOUR SON PRIVATE FIRST CLASS MORTON D
ELEVITCH WAS SERIOUSLY WOUNDED IN ACTION TWENTY EIGHT JANUARY
IN GERMANY MAIL ADDRESS FOLLOWS DIRECT FROM HOSPITAL W
```

February 7, 1945

FWANCE

Dear Peeples:

I was very glad to see Chaplain Buchanan from the 376th today—who assured me my glasses, pen & personal pictures and stuff were not lost as I had feared —I am now in a bigger better place—known as an evac hospital—now I'm just laying around waiting to be shipped to the ground, or convalescent hospital—

I'm about 700% better than at the time of my first letter written—only trouble is boredom—but days are passing faster—Usually start by washing up —then breakfast—sooner or later a cluster of captains come around clinging to a Lt Col., who examines the records and decides on what action should be taken—I had a Major Siegel operate on me back at the field hospital —nice guy—he was provoked because he was giving me a detailed account of his procedure in the operating room—and I fell asleep—

After laying around all day it feels good to get my back rubbed—Back at the field hospital I made the nurse try 80,675,432 different ways of rubbing until I got a slight resemblance to the way mom used to do—If your wondering —the only wounds on me was a small cut on the right upper arm and another on the right back—near the shoulder blade—no trouble at all—

[undated]

WHAT IS GOINK ON:

After a week of rest, we embarked on trucks fully equipted—happily wearing new snow hoods "Snow Pac" boots and double-canvas lined mittens.— Stopped for one peaceful night in a town—slept in our sleeping bags in a house—ate C-rations. Next day piled in trenches—slept in streaks—stood guard—huddled in holes covered with overcoats of dead Germans we'd dug up. Moved off next day with packs and my important ammo bag—struggled thru snow over hills—roads—thru woods—past bodies—under fire—puffed to a halt—crouched in muddy foxholes. Not for long—we were to be committed. Regretfully dumped our equip. in the middle of the woods, cautiously wound down snowy trails, cringing under whine of artillary. Frantically dug in whenever we stopped. Had on overcoats, belts, helmet, rifle, my 8 man squad got called on by Boomer—pushed thru some woods formed a line at edge of clearing. Silence was tense as it could be as Costello glided toward smoking enemy tank—trigger finger waited for reaction from brain— nothing happened—tank empty. But couldn't relax—sent to forward slope of hill to observe—watched our tanks and terrific battle—snow puff up and smudge back—mortars landed near us in clearing to our right—Brown and I sent back with messages—plunged thru woods—followed rabbit trail— Finally crashed out—ran under shells to C.P.—evidently drawing fire with high power radio—we'd rock down in unison—finally turned it off. P.O. talked calmly over walkie-talkie. Hawklike mess sgt was there on edge of hole —couldn't figure out why—rested at bazooka position—went back—we got a radio—couldn't make it work. Shortly moved out (in lead) to attack— streamed out across long open field and up long hill—no casualties—found tanks waiting—followed them as they smashed thru woods firing—many prisoners going back—one a women—abandoned German bazookas. Down across a road to a ditch—into more woods to contact Co. G. Find em—neck deep in shell holes. I find a luger by a tree—Bob Murlin unloads it. Stuffs it in his pocket as mine are bulging—"You can have it if I don't get out," I say. "You'll get out," he says. We go back out to ditch.

I watch more tanks lumber by — doughboys stream across snow below — craters bloom between some — they reach the town ahead of us — it is an inferno — many tanks shake after direct hits — they wheel and grind about — one commander starts back on foot — says he can do no more — another, his face like one out of a minstril show says "Not me — I still got bullets in this gun." Germans counter attack from woods at left — We build up line — tanks swing turret. Spray 50's at Nazis who resort to mortar and artillary. What's left of another co. starts thru woods to clear it — tanks never stop maneuvering. Colonel gallantly exposes himself — pounds on tanks to get 'em to "open up" and get directions — around town it looks like artist's painting of a battle — even colored flares! It is getting darker setting off the spectacle — we draw into woods again, to dig in in case of another counter attack — hear another battalion is being guided in to relieve us. I begin to notice mud and water have seeped over my body — strange tightness in head and stomach. We get relieved — moon out — back across road into ditch — my head toward town — leaders checking on men — start to depart. Hear dreadful seal sound of 120 mortar — "oop oop oop" — see orange flash 50 yds away. Feel burning in right arm. "I'm hit," I say. Brew in front of me — Murlin behind. "Get away from here," they say. I try to walk — whole right side pushing in — I think concussion has pulverized my insides — sink back in ditch on stomach — moan "I can't breathe."

Everyone leaves — alone with Brew. He sticks — shells still fall all around — "Doc" Spicer comes up — decides against morphine — goes for jeep. — I feel blood trickling in arm — ask for tourniquet — Brew runs all over looking for medics — takes bayonet, rips overcoat — dumps on sulfa — applies bandage to upper arm — sticks. Much later jeep creeps up — drag me out of ditch — long agonizing bumpy ride — Can't believe we're going back — keep seeing tanks all over the place — my feet are numb — I worry more about them than anything else. When I think I can't stand it any more we arrive at suffocatingly warm battalion aid — figures jut and loom above me — Chaplain Buchanan gives me hot soup thru a tube — they take my personal items — wish they hadn't — I learn I have 3 fractured ribs — talk freely — more maddening rides in ambulances — end up at field hospital.

Morphine has soothed me — joke and insult everyone including nurses — don't remember much — except protests as x-rays taken twice — on operating table — bright lights — ask for details — ether sends everyone floating away — Wake up naked between sheets — tubes in nose, chest and arm — feed me glucose and blood plasma for few days — plunge gallons of penicillin in left arm — I keep sliding down on pillows — have to be lifted up — never comfortable — lay on left side at night — cough continually — spit up red stuff—ask for morphine . . . helps me relax. Tubes come out one by one—get baths—get shaved. Howl worse then during any other time—a "Garcia from Texas" keeps killing me by digging his thumb in my neck—nurses are o.k. Get promised fruit juice—wait 8 hours—no go—see Chaplains, Majors, Colonels. Eat soft diet—then regular—surprized to find I can't eat—have to chew for hours before swallowing. Gaze at magazines—find out personal stuff is lost— show me hunk of shrapnel which lacerated lung, landed in diaphram. Get bundled up—ambulance ride to evac hosp. Lay around all afternoon, chest tapped at night. Use novacaine but can feel drill oscillate. Drain out 350 cc "straw colored liquid." My coughing stops. Finally get German-style "bed"— give me sleeping pills—instead I get "jag"—talk—fall asleep from exhaustion —in evac hosp few more days—more x-rays. Pretty nurse—bathe—shave myself—can't sit up yet—taken thru rain to tent—lay on asphalt floor. Hear tragic stories from other fellows—radio wails behind—miserable in narrow litter—tent leaking—in morning we hear planes—one comes in—gets stuck in mud—pulled out by doughs. We load on. I land by window—coffee and doughnuts from carefree gal—who unknowingly treats two PWs—marvel at beautiful uniforms of plane crew—take off—smoothly—ride is amazing—we glide and float along—noise noticeable—we ride clouds—watch France slide by below—swoop down on Paris—thru crowded streets—past cafes—to another evac hosp. Lay around couple more days. French wardboys and ladies get all directions mixed up—try to be helpful—strange patients—one like a rag doll entire head and hands bandaged. Man with thick black glasses announces show: "Your attention please. I am happy to present a show for you this afternoon. Don't mistake this cockney accent—I'm really French— Unfortunately our beautiful girl singer is ill with bronchitis and can't appear. The other male in the show is reluctant to perform without her—so that leaves me. Well, I'm an organist by trade. But as yet I haven't been able to locate one. Therefore I must bid you goodbye. It's been a pleasure entertaining you."

Ambulances thru rain again to planes—load on and again get window— Find two other guys from old 7th Co. at Benning on with me—Taxi far down past many sights—take off at green light—roll thru storms and brilliant sunlight—France is patched and shadowed under the clouds—I'm convinced air travel is for me—The channel is deep blue—see other planes—thicken over Britain—white cliffs—farms—roads—houses—panorama even greater than "The Boulevard"—circle finally—come in—more ambulances—over hills to cluster of tiny curved dome buildings—land in beautiful bed—white sheets—white blankets—weather strange—snows—move out again next morn in "limy" ambulance—big and bulky as a box car—Greeted at Gen. Hosp. Fill out forms. Still have box of personal stuff—wallet—x-rays—

assigned to pleasant ward two, three stoves—warm—nice beds—all
recreational facilities desired—PX—library—hope to get shoes this aft.
Go get writing stuff—shaving cream. Got bath towel—wash my hair later—
cut yesterday—wrote back for personal junk—account of most terrible week
in my life was written twice before—will repeat same and send—so many
guys are dead now I wrote of all the time—even Fanset and Ellicott—bigger
shocks to come—I am a very lucky man—Gadding about here in luxury—
"Stars and Stripes" few days ago had picture and appropriate caption—
particularly significant to me—I see no reason for it being omitted—but if so
I'd appreciate censor returning it to me. As you realize, I haven't had mail in
ages—send much now to my new address—I should be here long enough to
receive it. Nothing to do but few exercises and clean up details—sun out again
today. For the record—I was operated on by a Maj. Arnold Siegal—nice guy—
my stitches are already out—everything shipshape. Reading "Esquire," "Bear
Facts" Digest—and "Goodnight Sweet Prince," Fowler's masterpiece—

Goombye

Mort

February 20

ENGLAND

Pepe:

Today I pushed the sheets away to stare at a sunny morn. When the windows
were opened I saw England again—practically the same natural scenes I left
six months ago—The green grass waved and the stone walls loped past the
hilly checkerboards of green, gray and brown where cows and streams moved
contentedly—The gray strip of road and perpendicular gray columns of trees
inserted the usual geometrical pattern—but of main importance was the blue
sky and the sun gleaming on my cigar-shaped sanitarium—I left it today for
the first time under my own power—The captain decided to permit me to
eat chow at the mess hall—whereupon I was given a pair of shoes and a
convalescent suit—to wander about—waddled forth on an excursion with
Katz just as general and yes men arrived—gazed upon him and a sunlit
valley to my right—decided it was just another Grant Wood and inverted my
nostrils to avoid colliding with the PX—having received my allotment Sunday,
I beetled down past a bah-bah shop, post office, surgery—to the library—the
library is so diminutive the bookworms must be born roundshouldered—Soon
I was freezing in the prickling air and wheezing up the Santa Fe trail past the

mess hall, theater to my final object—the crimson Red Cross—By now
I was rasping in glee—noting my head was in a slight whirl—accomplished
something by finding my ready-to-mail Purple Heart—staggered up the hill
to ward 2—my back and arm felt like they were asleep—"Every step is doing
you good" Katz said, supporting my weight on his arm.

Home again, I decided to write you, and fell into a reflecting daze—British
operator borrows my book to raise the machine—2½ hrs later I claim it. "You
were on page 236" he says—upon examining my x-rays last week I discovered
one rib was missing: no 7. I worry about things like that—

Sunday a Mexican strolled up to my bed with a chess board. Immediately
I pictured long-haired be-spectacled introverts meditating motionless over
a sea of wood chips; grudgingly consented to soak up directions—when he
completed the nomenclature and asked if I understood I wisely failed to
answer—instead asked him to start the game, hoping it would compensate
him for his patience and good intentions—as I moved a "pawn" I thought of
my 23 straight losses in checkers—soon learned which way each piece could
move; astounded him by winning decisively; promised dejected swarthy one
another contest—Yesterday we moved to his bed. I moved cautiously but
made mistakes—finally check-mated his king in swift maneuver—trouble
was he had to tell me I had won! Naturally I felt like a rodent.

February 21, 1945   Dept. of Patients 4152
                                               U.S. Army Hosp. Plant

Orchid Dew:

The last two days have been adventuresome—I expanded my chest in chill—
sunny air—and saw the real English landscape again—You see I have been
endowed with shoes and a convelescent suit, involving pants and a jacket—
windproof against Britains refreshing bitters—All this is encountered en route
to the mess-hall, a clamorous but satisfying refuge at meal time—returned
from breakfast with a lumpy cargo of Sunkist seedless oranges! My travels
left me (in the company of Katz) to the PX, Bahbah shop, post office, library
and Red Cross—Got my Purple Heart and it's ready to mail—Now that
my bandages are off—I can take a shower,—Twill feel good—My eyes are
standing up well under a rigid non-tiring program. Oh yes—played another
game of chess—sad fact was I won it too—on his bed! Just in case I dont get
my glasses you might inquire at T.P. Optical to see if they have the formula—

February 24

Ramon:

Two nights ago I sat in a theater—saw Warner Bros "The Animal Kingdom"—first such enjoyable evening since that eerie night in Germany when we first-nighters hustled thru the shadows—It seems I have a pneumothorax—which as I see it—is an air pocket in the lung chamber—to remove same—doc inserts ⅝" needle bearing novacane, attached to machine—Chess is still wasting my hours—

February

U.S. Army Hospital
Cirencester, England

Recalcitrant Nymph:

A month ago today I was slogging through snow-capped mud, concerned about not much more than the bobbing back ahead, guiding me thru death-pale air to a ditch where rifle no.783324 would fall to rust, and my fingerprints would fade in the battle haze—In this past month my reincarnation has been complete—complete enough so my brain propels my pencil to such as the above—and refuses to accept the facts as nothing more than a fantasy—a dream—which could become very real again—

February 28
England

[V-Mail]

Violet Sparrow—

Here I am reading other peoples' mail (as usual). I remember sitting on Fanset's bed reading his mail, while he puzzled over Burr's—I haven't mentioned it before—but Fanset is dead—When last I saw him, we were striding side-by-side among ghostly forms on a pale white road—We were to attack at dawn, but you'd hardly know it—The laughter and joking were so loud. I'd been drawing apart from John W., since he was in a weapons platoon. But now it was the same as ever. As he reminded me of the story of "The Two Blue Gnus and the Yak" I used to tell in Georgia—No time though; we were winding up a narrow trail in the woods toward smoke and death, and he plunged ahead to deliver machine gun ammo where it was needed . . .

Mort

March 2

Tiger Tongue:

The kitchen has me in its clutches again, but this time I don't have to wade in the mud and scrub pots and pans in the rain—instead we have all the modern conveniences in our cozy nook—where we serve food in shining silver trays to the bed patients—FLASH!—Sitting here writing, when a guy asks me if I want to be in a radio show! I have visions of Piccadilly Circus, but it so happens they bring the mike right in the ward—he says it's the "Bebe Daniels show" over Mutual—March 11—sort of a birthday present [to mother] wot? (Hope I aint put a yami on it)

> Dept of Patients
> US Army Hosp Plant

March 4, 1945

[V-Mail]

Cucoon Fuzz:

Feeling extremely benevolent (?) I reestablished my advice to the love-lorn; succeeded in drawing out a misguided youth who desired to sever intimate relations with a female; discovered he was a cad, a bounder and a chaplin; helped him turn out a letter that will undoubtedly drive the girl to suicide ..

> Dept of Patients
> US Army Hospital

Cirencester, England

March 6, 1945

CONCERTO FOR TWO SPOONS

"You lose, Pustis." Lazo was dangling his frail fingers before Barnes' smoldering green eyes. "I move here, you move there, I go there, you have to push rookie there, I yell CHACKING—you rush up with a pawn, and it's MATE!" With the last violent ejaculation, he swept the trembling players off the board and slowly slipped senseless to the floor, happily frothing and bobbing his head against the bed. "El moto car-EE," buzzed Barnes, slapping the gaunt frame below him, "let's go to chow!"

I met them at the hallway entrance, where I was hugging the doorway under a banging loud speaker thru which occasional piano chords could be discerned. "Rachmaninoff," I whispered. "My brother's got an album of it at home." Overcome with emotion Barnes wheeled and savagely read off the daily bulletin in gutteral German. Large, salty tears manipulated the pimply route to his puffy darting tongue. Lazo was gathering himself for a rush. "Chow?" he gibbered, dashing into the corridor and eventually the nurse's cart. Emerging from the hemostats, ether and sterilized gauze, he discovered his left arm in a grip of molybdenum steel, which was slowly twisting if off like a soggy chicken wing. "El moto car-ee!" Barnes grimaced. "Can't you listen to this purely for culture's sake? You can eat three times a day but you can hear this only once." "Yes," I whispered, "Rachmaninoff—My brother's got an album of it at home."

I began waving my arms, little noticing the two pokers and a coal shovel I had dropped. [I was on stove detail.] Fellows were going to chow. Katz and Sauceda came rushing up. "Mathematics is an exact science," shouted Sauceda. "I can take two apples and two apples and have four—but take chemistry—the formulas never come out exactly right—" "Look here," I moaned, accidentally jabbing Lazo in the empiena, "didn't Guy Lussac or Lavosier or somebody prove the laws of chemical changes?" "Your calendar," Katz prompted, viewing with fascination the bubbling asphalt surrounding the large poker. "We're going to change the time system—100 seconds in an hour, 20 hours in a day, 9 days in a week, 10 weeks in a month—"

Lazo was quivering: "Chow, chow, chow, chow! I want to discuss the setting up of a socialistic regime in Guatemala!" "It'll end soon," I assured him. "The end's the best—sends shivers up and down your spine. Rachmaninoff, you know; my brother's got an album of it at home."

At that moment the final spasmotic notes of the concerto bounded down among us, accompanied by a terrific sensation on the epidermis (posterior). My flushed countenance traced a misguided stream of icy water to a faucet, expertly jammed by Katz' forefinger. "The floor," he gasped. "Getting a bit sticky, you know."

Barnes was in the corridor. We meekly formed a column behind him, voicing our enthusiastic approval of the great piano composition. "Rachmaninoff," I whispered. "My brother's got it in an album at home."

March 23, 1945

ABZSC [brother] —

Got our pass for 0800 March 21 — but I couldn't find a necktie — so we wasted some time — Jesus (He-soos) Sauceda, who I went with, ranted all morn about my stupidity — we get out to the gate and he remembers he forgot his money . .

We make a complete tour of Cirencester in six minutes — It is not long before a kindly old lady give us printed spiritual messages — which make excellent confetti —

On the train we decide we need liquid more than donuts and relieve a cocker spaniel of a bowl of milk — In Kimbal we switch to the London train (Great Western) and ride along looking at the backs of papers people are reading — The pictures are revealing, since the English have a sensible outlook on life, and don't mind seeing themselves —

In London we narrowly miss being run over ten times, which is most unusual, having crossed streets eleven times . . The street lights in London have been abandoned in their original capacity — They now serve as tests for color blindness — A bobby gives us easy directions to the Strand — "Second right," he says, "second right, turn left, third right cut thru an alley, go thru a tunnel, kiss the Blarny Stone six times, snap your fingers — CAWNT MISST"

Our trail of sweat leads us to "Abie's Gin Joint," a fashionable rendezvous, boycotted by pedestrians — we attempt to signal them, appealing to their hospitality — true, they don't look at us — finally Jesus rolls a pebble down an old man's earphone, and he takes us into his confidence —

The visit to the Savoy was nothing but a ride in the swinging doors . . We lurch in a little joint where we obtain an order of the old standby fish and chips. Most satisfying — "Aged in the wood" must apply to fish caught in the bilge of a ship . .

"Arsenic and Old Lace" was far superior to anything I saw or could have imagined in the States — the cast looked like it had been sitting around year after year waiting for that play to be written — Between acts tea and buttered tea [sic] were served but we were too busy discussing the play and plotting seat locations of women we'd noticed . . "Teddy" — was magnificent — He is looking like Theodore Roosevelt — "Deelighted" he is saying, "Deee-lighted" — on the upper landing of the stairs a light shines on his face — He waves his arms — "SHAWGE!"

Jesus wants beer — I drag him all over but always the tuxedoes change our mind — The Gay Paree aint where it usta be — we ask a guy where we can find a place to eat. "Second right" he says, "second right, turn left, third right, cut thru an alley, go thru a tunnel, kiss the Blarny Stone six times, snap your fingers—CAWNT MISST"

The Red Cross served a fair breakfast.

Mort

[undated fragment]
. . . Inside is usual smelly mob with watery eyes and nicotine lips—But there is noticeable lack of G.I.s—This friend of mine is chinning with two woebegone damsels, and I linger nearby getting shoved in the back by a waiter with mugs yelling "Henkyo!" The door is opening and closing and I am catching glimpse of startling female in corridor—I ease out thar—what is this, I wonder—a girl with brown flashing eyes—nice complexion, figure, clothes—in <u>hyar</u>? She is wearing green kerchief on brownish hair and a dark coat and is generally giving impression of most frail, beautious females I see in London but I am too stupid to speak to—then something abnormal happens: I speak to she—and continue doing so with much ease.—This sounds ridiculous—but for Morton is great step—Hideous childer crowd 'bout begging, clawing, drooling—we go outside—This girl has been stood up by an English paratrooper—and altho' she denies it she is looking for him, she is—Meanwhile we—or rather I am talking—experimenting with this new pastime to the utmost—it is pleasant—because for some strange reason Morton has acquired a "typing" eye—and this doll is suiting him more than somewhat—being she is intelligent, rather quiet —and does not drink—However—I do notice the brown stain on the fingers —but say nothing—It has been a long time since I talk to anyone with brains—so I discourse freely on everything—tending to show her I am a "different" Yank—For some reason she stays with me—and I glare back at other GIs who are sizing she up and are suggesting I go in and have a drink— The beeg test comes when she meets another English paratrooper and declines his offer to allow me to walk home wit her! Hmm—so I taking her home to one of the red brick buildings bunched all over the place—naturally I think of such things as holding of the . . .

DANIELS:

ELLEVITCH:

DANIELS:

ELLEVITCH:

DANIELS:

Dear Mrs. Elevitch,

This is just a short note to say that I saw your son and he was looking very well.

I hope you heard the broadcast over Mutual Network, that it came over clearly and that you were notified to listen in. Please let me know if by chance you were not notified, otherwise please don't bother to answer as I know you are satisfied in hearing your son's voice.

With kindest regards,
I remain,
Sincerely,

Bebe Daniels.

ELLEVITCH: I WAS WITH THE 94TH INFANTRY DIVISION IN THE SAAR
ATTACK
TRIANGLE. WE'D BEEN ON A THREE DAY OPERATION AND I'D
GONE THROUGH WITHOUT A SCRATCH. THEN JUST AS WE WERE
BEING RELIEVED THE GERMANS STARTED SENDING SHELLS AT
GOT RATHER INTIMATE WITH ME
US AND ONE OF THEM HAD MY SERIAL NUMBER ON IT.

DANIELS: THAT WAS TOUGH LUCK. WHAT HIT YOU, AN 88?

ELLEVITCH: NO. IT WAS A 120 MM MORTAR SHELL. YOU KNOW WHAT THOSE
SOUND LIKE, DON'T YOU BEBE?

DANIELS: YES BUT I'D LIKE TO HEAR YOUR DESCRIPTION.
SEAL WITH A MILD CASE OF
LARYNGITIS
ELLEVITCH: WELL IF YOU HEAR A NOISE LIKE A LOT OF SEALS BARKING ,
EXPECT
YOU CAN LOOK OUT FOR 120 MM MORTAR SHELLS.

DANIELS: THEY'RE VICIOUS THINGS. BUT YOU'RE DOING ALRIGHT NOW,
AREN'T YOU MORT?

ELLEVITCH: YES I'M FEELING FINE AND I GUESS IT WON'T BE LONG BEFORE
I'M OUT AND ABOUT AGAIN.

DANIELS: THAT'S FINE. WELL GOOD LUCK TO YOU FELLOW.

April 3

NOTE NEW ADDRESS—
    Co D—Dept of Patients 4167
    US Army Hosp Plant APO 118

This is the type of story that makes sentimentals like you and me shed tears—
a few minutes ago I am wandering out of a messhall, and somebody is coming
up to me and saying "Hello" He is on KP and is ridiculous looking but he is
SIDNEY ELLICOTT!! "You is dead!" I say. "I say, really?" he says—Then I mumble
away forgetting to wash my mess kit—was going to write beeg letters—but
will probably spend all nite talking to he—had nice train ride up hyar—
hospital isnt bad—but training—? Rush mail to I plizz

Mottn

V-MAIL

April 11, 1945

From: Pfc Harry C Francisco	To: Pfc Morton Elevitch
Co A 376th Inf	Dept of Pts., 4152
Germany	US Army Hospital Plant

How are you getting along. I hope that they're doing OK. Your wounds I
mean. Plenty of Penicillin shots no doubt.
    Andy Rothenback wants me to ask you if you have a copy of that story
that you wrote on Butzdorf ["IT"]. We are still trying to get that Presidential
Citation for the company and that story would help.* Please send us a copy if
you can.

Your friend

Cisco

April 15, 1945

ENGLAND

Koroad:

On this auspicious occasion I am playing the sniveling wretch—"A" Company
is marching off to town to precipitate in the Roosevelt matrimonies. Therefore,
"D" Company is having K.P., meaning it is falling upon my broad clavicles.

*We did receive the Citation.

But this is not too bad—as I have completed my mourning work and write this to you while peoples eat—

Last even I am embarking off to town with Ellicott, Flick and Mason. This town is large and noted for its beauty—However, much has been smudged by the blitz—We are waiting in line dodging moisture globules when the busses are commencing to stop while the drivers eat—We drop in a mess hall and divulge in some sandwiches—First thing I do in this community is purchase a ticket to Thornton Wilder's "The Skin of Our Teeth" with Vivien Leigh. Now I must cross my teeth. I mean fingers. So that I will not again land upon a detail —If I do I will go straight to the company commander, then straight to the kitchen. Next we must find a bed for Mason, who is on a 24 hr pass—We are locating the Salvation Army, a bee-hive of old men with dirty cracked cups and brown stained collars—The boys are desiring things to eat—we are wandering hither and hather and they are pushing into a pub for a bit of ale. We sit around a wet red table, poking our reddening faces above flurries of smoke and laugh spray—Beer after beer is arriving and disappearing, and the boys are becoming quite jovial indeed—They are pouring dozens of cigarettes and chiclets around—and are broadcasting their presence no little. Ellicott is the same as ever—jerky, nervous, red-eyed and repentant at the ribaldness of the spectacle. Flick is showering conversation on four horrible hags and is constantly removing and inserting a plate of tooth under cover of his musty pulled-up field jacket. Mason is just glossy about the optic organs. I am disremembering to tell you of chips which we buy before we enter the pub. They are hot and greasy and full of vinegar and are gradually dissipating before us in the alcoholic aroma—

The main purpose in mind is to attend a dance which is held in "Neal's Ballroom"—I herd the gentlemen out and smilingly totter longside Sidnith. Little gamin children are swarming about us as usual demanding things I aint got and wouldnt give 'em if I did have anyway. They paw desperately at each of us. They whirl away as someone flings something used [condom] out of a doorway. Flick fades off the curb in the path of a pretty girl on a bicycle. He manages to escape a treaded head due to our alertness—We finally get on a bus that deposits us under a bridge. A train trundles over our heads blowing us into a series of face contortions. We are patronizing numerous excretory implements, one of which is behind a bawdy pub. In we go, watch limpid-eyed limeys play a strange variety of billiards. Ellicott knows he shouldn't drink more, but does of course. Mason has spied something in blue with bumps and decides to part company with us—About 2110 we find "Neal's" and I hand out 3 shillings thrice—Female women of the opposite sex distribute themselves thickly—only recorded music retains the misty motion, as the band rests—Ellicott and Flick leer about—"We always go up on the balcony before," they say, "but tonight we get drunk so we will go right out on the floor"—

Up on the balcony, Ellicott and Flick leer about.

Presently a green and brown dress sits down. I save the table while the advance guards move out. "This is Betsy," Flick says, "and this is Edna."—They go downstairs—Ellicott comes up with Edna, who is excusing herself—"She stood me up," Ellicott says fifteen minutes later as we watch Bob bobbing below. But Flick is bringing Betsy and Edna back—Edna sits beside me. She has brown hair, brown eyes and a face that fluctuates with my facetiousness— As Ellicott has observed, she is someone who is what we do not figure to find in such affairs. She would rather stay in the balcony and conwoice on matters. She is inquiring as to my interests and I rattle off with the usual which delights her no little, especially when I bring in "my mother sang in opera"— so we talk about Dickens and Shakespeare etc.

Meanwhile the time is slipping to 2210 and I am horrified as I remember the other two men are down on the floor totally unprotected. I find Ellicott mouthing orange soda with a mound of polka dots with sores on her legs. "Where did you produce that?" I inquire later. "She cut in on me," he says— So we all get together again on the balcony—Ellicott is getting everybody's names mixed up introducing people to his new find, a lichen named Iris— But I drag them away. "One more dance," says Ellicott, "I'll rap yuh, rap yuh, rap yuh"—Flick doesnt quite do what he wants to do with Betsy, but he is indignant because she doesnt jitterbug. Out in lovely air again, I find we have ten minutes to reach the bus line. I leave my fondlings joining company with a guy who leads me a merry chase cross town. I am worried to pieces but cleverly buck the line—Tuther two stagger in, I see them in the glare of headlights and give them a hail.

This place is crawling with cruising women who intercept the flailing faces of inebriated ones—A pretty mess it is. All dashes from skirt to skirt are loudly approved by the lengthening line. It is a fitting climax to all this, and I am glad to drop in bed at 2230—So at 0500 they wake me. Some coincidence —the day I arrive Ellicott is on K.P. (outside) . . The day he leaves I am on K.P. (inside).

Yes, Sidnith is leaving. Slobslob—

I'm in the Red Cross now—after a shower—the radio brings us details on Franklin Roosevelt being laid to rest—This is sadness to be sure—The shock is wearing off but the effect will never leave. For my present mood—I better get mail soon to pull me up <u>pliz</u> . . At the moment I am wearing my new glasses which pawpaw sent — they fit perfectly — Taps hush the room — being a sentimental person I hesitate to stop my pencil for tears would come — Fortunately we can still have our thoughts — All these days flutter and fade — Something makes me feel as if I'd swallowed a cockroach. Jim Nance from "A" Co just sat down. Started writing this after I finished an attempted (not yet completed) conversation with "that's the trouble with the army, you never know what'll happen next."

April 25, 1945

ENGLAND

Gosling —

Where did you get the idea that Ellicott was disfigured?? He was perfectly o.k. —just sprained his arm jumping into a foxhole — Got sent all the way back here — as the doctors thot it was broken (!?) He's had his seven day, delay-en-route — spent Sunday with him 'fore he left for the replacement center — . . Dont be compelled to send me all the news — we usually here of it before you do

Helped patch a fence this morning —

Took another bouncy truck ride to Stratford upon-Avon — in the co. of a goggle-eyed pimple puss who draws "crazy virgins" and a lanky guy from Mpls name o' "Shadow" . . We hadnt had supper — so strode thru the cobble-stone streets to the ancient well-preserved "White Swan Hotel" . . Stratford has modern stores but the buildings of the Shakespearean age have been retained and far outnumber the new — every business is a "Shakespeare" something or other — written in old English script — The tiny windows, thatched roofs & green lawns have a musty air, but the squawking British autos pull us out of the poetic reverie — Supper consisted of fish and chips, squares of bread, salad, jam on pie crust and coffee — with this we were content to slouch in the Shakespeare memorial theater and watch "Othello"

May 2, 1945

ENGLAND

Gainsborough:

This letter you write to me April 24 is getting me all worried about this Mrs. Fanset business again — I explain once why I cannot write upon she — If she is making fresh demands I will comply—But surely you realize it is over three months already and I am no Ghoul . . . I would much rather see her in person —To you one little letter must seem mighty simple—and to her mighty important—but this boy in question is like an image to me, and cannot be dispensed with so easily—I cannot say "He died smiling," for I know he did not . . . But once more I feebly say "I'LL TRY" . . .

May 2, 1945

ENGLAND

Tamatonsky—

Radio announced surrender of Germans in Italy—Went over to "K" Co barber shop tother day—but the power was off—Sat in a darkened place 'round a stove—listened—guys were talking about their future—world's future—why can't I transcribe this—I thought—people should hear things like this—lot o' things would be clearer—

May 8, 1945

ENGLAND

VE Day!

Shaddrac:

There may have been a lull in your mail since the lettre I mailed May 4 came back—This is the first place since I've been in the army that has returned mail to me—But more than that the same type of lettre has passed by this place half a dozen times before (???) . . L called last week—and as arranged—we met—He had a bicycle which interfered no little—Finally checked it. In muggy weather we ventured to "The large city" and got a good start by finding a nice

Evening De

No. 16,788.   *Lighting-up time; 10.43 p.m.*   MONDAY, 7 MAY, 1945.

IT'S OVER!

TO-MORROW WILL BE V-DAY

Churchill and The King to broadcast

V-DAY WILL BE TO-MORROW. THE PRIME MINISTER WILL BROADCAST AT 3 O'CLOCK TO-MORROW AFTERNOON AND THE KING AT 9 p.m

hotel room, which wealthy L paid for — From there we wandered around
town, seeing "It's all Over" in red headlines — Bunting and flags being hung
out — Presently ate — relaxed in the beautious Odeon Theatre — saw "Wilson"
— strangely appropriate for the moment — went to a nice park — met a girl
from Wales — little town name of llanfairpwllgwyngyllgogerychwyrnd-
robwlllanoysilioogogoch That is the name (It's very easy to pronounce) She
taught school — 50 ten year olds in fact — and is quite impressed with L "Her
Genius" — He is stepping into high gear and is capturing her completely by the
time we reach her home — Downtown a regular riot is ensuing and we mingle
at our own risk. With the crowd — L is accumulating lipstick — lovely night —
as it were — but it rains this morn — Free breakfast at Red Cross — Big doings
out hyer — Women all over d' place — Band — Guess what — I'm K.P.
tomorrow — But another pass may result —

—Soldier's Saga—
or "A Dream Walking"

Now that there has been a slight easing of censorship regulations in this
theatre — I can balance the books — as it were — to you the dates and names
won't mean much — but it will help complete the file of information that has
been accumulating, and will help clarify the many letters by binding them
together into sort of a "Dream" story. Now I am ready to push off again into a
new series of experiences — the last ten months I've been wandering about in
a haze, realizing more and more the hopelessness of the army and appreciating
the freedom I didn't have. But the recent months have given me a chance to
rest and think — many things I haven't told you, and will delay revealing until
my return. I am no psychoneurotic case — I am merely patiently sitting in a
steam bath, waiting for the excess burden to drop off —

After a dusty train ride thru southern states we arrived at Camp Shanks,
New York on July 27, 1944. Soon we "camels" found ourselves on the magnificent "Queen Elizabeth" — and greeted the shores of Scotland on August 12
after a swift six-day voyage. It was the greenness and beauty of Greenoch that
I described to you. On a joltless "toy" train we passed thru soft-hued Scotland,
stopped at Carlisle and deposited our burden of equipment and clothes in
frosty-cold southern England for a month. We endured savage slashes of
sun and rain, living in six-man tents and mud — we had slightly revised the
grounds, the residence of Queen Mary, known as "Pinckney Park." I told
you of my visits to Gloucester and Bristol and London. But this was all a
preparation for bigger things. After a field problem out at the "Hill with the

Green Glade on Top" we packed up once more. At that time air power was astounding . . . We used to watch the huge air fleets passing overhead, endless red, green and yellow lights at night, sparkling flashes in the morning sunlight. We could hear them as we trudged down to the train that took us to Southampton. On a drizzly morning we filed up the gangplank of "The Chesire" to brave the channel crossing. It was on this ship that the Hindus did their gigantic swindling business I told you about.

On Sept. 10 we tested the sand of "Utah Beach," still crawling with pillboxes, "minen" and untouched bodies. Here began the most strenuous ordeal I have yet undergone—the march inland with our huge packs—thru mud, rain and blackness. Next morn we rose stiff and numb in the "cow pasture"—you know the story from there—I had my first hot shower in Rennes—we were outside the city in "The Apple Orchard"—Our first taste of combat came after "that truck ride" to Temple—It was there that I was sent to form the General's Guard—The scene of the "Consternation" story was Heric, France. The story of "The Delightful Ride" came later on as we moved near La Paqueles. We still attended those movies at Heric, however.

All this time I was in the St. Nazaire sector making passes to Nantes possible—when I returned to Co. A around Nov. 18 I found them outside of Hennebont in the Lorient sector—We soon moved into a muddy rest area—then took up positions facing german-held Kervignac. I used to write you squatting on my helmet watching our boys shoot at snipers in the buildings—from this "Leaning Forest" area we went to those lovely German barracks, where the pictures were taken—then back to the big camp near Rennes—where I was Christmas.

But New Year's Day found us in holes again near Blaine—We weren't there very long. We moved to an assembly area at Chateaubriant, preparing for our ride to Germany—I told you of our pup-tent city wheezing under a snow storm. The miserable "40 and 8" car ride was interrupted several times by stops for coffee and doughnuts, once at Lemans, once south of Paris—We were originally scheduled for "SHAEF" reserve at Reims, but somewhere between Metz and Nancy we were re-routed and hit the snow near Thionville. Trucks took us to Perl, Germany, where my squad occupied "P. Bucken's" town hall. It was a wonderful week, but the lightening hit us with the announcement on Jan. 12 that "we attack at dawn"—The following attack on Tettengen and Butzdorf resulted in the most terrible week in my existence. It was here that Fanset and Walters were killed and I first experienced the dread sensation of utter hopelessness. I have written the whole story twice, but the letters are still in Germany.

When we dragged into Wochern, cold, wet, weary but safe, I wondered why I was alive. Then you'll remember my letters said "France" again. It was actually St. Francois in Alsace-Lorraine. It was a week of recovery. But brought me nearer to my last attack. During this week we had A-1 priority on showers, movies and special USO shows, since our unit had "been given up for lost," had nevertheless knocked out 15 tanks of the 11th Panzer division, and had escaped with a small loss of lives in comparison to the 900 Germans which were gathering snowflakes about Butzdorf.

The day after I mailed you my package we moved to Besch, Germany. Then toiled towards Sinz, sleeping in tank traps. If Burr hasn't shown you the story of the Sinz attack he can now—It was over for me on the third day. I was hit by 120 mortar fragments while lying in a ditch facing the flaming town. I finally ended up outside of Perl in a field hospital, where a foreign body was removed from my diaphram, after lacerating the pleura and lung, and smashing four ribs.

Eight days later I was preparing for a flight to Paris. We left Thionville, circled the Moselle River, and landed in Paris. On Feb. 10 I was back in England—over three months have passed, the most pleasant months in the army. The continent won't look good to me—but I can only hope that it will eventually culminate in a trip back home—

May 12

STATEMENT OF STATUS

This morning I pushed the button to launch myself on a period of puzzlement, wonder, and hope—Now that the war has ended my stay here has come to an abrupt end—The Lt. began to dictate—"Discharged to duty"—assignment limitations—no carrying pack, no hiking, no K.P., no heavy duty"—I asked if I could return to my outfit in that capacity—maybe I shouldnt have asked —for he changed the above to B-3-4-4x—meaning I shall return to the address you used before I entered a hospital—Utmost in importance is my return to the states—If I had been assigned to a limited assignment of service outfit it prob'ly would have meant a trip to the South Pacific—now I can only hope that the 94th will return to the states for re-organization—Don't worry —I understand my physical condition—soon I'll leave on a 7 day "delay-en-route" planning to visit Glasgow, Edinburgh and London—

May 17

ENGLAND

UBRT—

Harkin was my doctor—used to mutter everytime he'd see my operation—
"Who did dat," he'd ask—"Major Arnold Segal, 30th Field"—I'd whimper—
"Pretty good job," he'd muse, crinkling his chin—(but I'm the greatest chest
surgeon in the world; I'd have done better) He'd demonstrate the various
insisions on patients to visitors by vigourously yanking off the tape (and skin)
He'd jab his heart patients on the chest—"Healing up isn't it?" "Yessir," they'd
choke between tears—one guy with a bullet in his heart was out walking two
days after the operation—When Harkin came in the guy would have to stand
quivering by his bed, and raise his arms—But Harkin got results—He saved
lives—

Played a "Master of chess" last nite—Beat him thrice—Poor guy was quite
dejected—Got the book "The Razor's Edge" from a guy next to me—

Slong

May 26, 1945

ENGLAND

Recollections
of El Trippe

(I) Food—Most of the time I ate in the Red Cross—or guzzled cokes there—
had ice cream in Glasgow where fresh lettuce and salads were abundant—
even had a lettuce and tomatoe sandwich in London—Ate sticky pancakes for
breakfast at the Interstate Club—down in the Stagedoor Canteen (London)
they served waffles and jam topped with ice cream—On a train to Lichfield
four ladies fully occupying two eight foot seats passed "sweets" around
liberally—everywhere people eat ice cream sandwiches, loudly licking their
fingers—But Spam and powdered eggs still are featured in all the stores—

(II) Luxurys—Almost every nite I had a hot shower, clean towel, sheets—
I carried my stuff in an empty gas bag—First morning in Glasgow I had a
good haircut by a wee barber—Instead of raising the chair he had to tilt
it back so he could reach my hair—

(III) Recreation, etc. . . . . Trip to Balloch and Loch Lomund Park was on a
double-decker bus—Two small boys sat next to me—never asked for gum—

on the coming back a woman bothered me—all she said was "Heh" (?)—
People in Scotland volunteered information—they didnt say "You cawnt
misst" either—The Sunday morning stroll in Edinburgh was refreshing—
no movies or theaters are open on Sundays—Instead people queue to hear
lectures—A statue of Abe Lincoln is in Calton Cemetery—not many people
in kilts—One teen age boy accompanied his mother—both in bright skirts—
surprized that Sir Walter Scott got such a stupendous monument—his statue
is in white marble—The orators were out on Sunday too—got a picture of
'em—one white haired guy talks to the air—

London had more attractions—I was happy to notice that sandbags are
being removed from statues in Piccadilly Circus—and approaching the
mall—workman are also busy restoring the Abbey to its former beauty—It
seemed that I did a lot of walking—but something in a big city—The roaring
stream of vehicles and people—attracts me—The first morning walk took me
to the Palace—here thousands of people stood about watching the formal
change of guard—I snapped a picture of the band leading the old guard out
the gate in slow-step time—Up at Westminster Bridge I found more crowds—
all waiting for the German U-boat to come in—It finally did—and curious
heads poked about—I hated to go in at night—but had nothing else to do—
G.I.s swarm all over the place—the people are showing their influence by
using our phrases excessively—"Are you kidding?"—"What's cooking?" "Me
ayekin Bock"—Dogs are very smart and popular and usually a cluster of them
on leashes peer out the rear door of the trams—English cigarettes come in all
size boxes and packages—it is not uncommon to see men and women with a
nicotine stained fingers—The butts are smoked so far down that thumb and
forefinger must be inserted between the lips to remove them—London is
returning to peacetime—Vets in blue suits and red ties are everywhere
—the pubs are packed and forms murmur in doorways—

(IV)—St James Park—As I've seen before—I spent much time here—
The park is filled all day long—People just sitting—Tuppence is collected for
water side seats—wealthy-looking business men stride along—Big Ben drones
the hours two blocks away—swans glide in the shadows—Ducks sputter and
splash—of chief interest was a family of ten wee ducklets and their mother—
standing on a bridge you get a view of the shimmery-calm water—low
hanging trees with white buildings rising beyond—Doing nothing in
such a place is not a waste of time—

Mort

Today has been uneventful—gloomy out—I washed some clothes—read magazines—hard to say what is ahead—But my days in England are limited—

May 30, 1945

England

Gnonnm

Few more scraps of paper to get rid of—Been on guard duty today—as supernumerary—Had it fairly easy—camp here is clearing out—so we'll be leaving too—Heard that my outfit is in the army of occupation—Now it looks as tho I wont return altho' the latter deal would be better than going to the South Pacific under any circumstances—Finished a "Treasury of Science"—very enlightening on the miracle of life—since I met "Jesus" at the 160th I've been interested in evolution and genetics!

May 31, 1945

This morning I come off guard, go to Lichfield for interview with callassification officer—special services division—He is wondering whether I would be interested in information-education-program, giving lectures—I dont say much—then he asks me about my cartooning, acting, says
        maybe I oughta be in special services—

June 6, 1945

England

Lapre . .

Today is a busy one—and reluctant I am to see it pass—I am in chair outside of theatre which is now ge-filt with rows and rows of packs and duffle bags—Late-late tonite we'll load ourselves in trains and soon we'll be chuffin' cross the channel—

5

The Guardsman:
France, June–December 1945

We are waiting for the monster of an army to disband.

June 16, 1945

CHARTRES, FRANCE

HAMMER MY KNEE

. . You must have followed my frustrated excursions to the 19th Rein. Depot, where I get slapped with an assignment to a signal service outfit—which, as I dope it, is merely a way of disposing of unwanted hordes of men—They are unwanted in the repo depo—unneeded in the ETO—but nevertheless retained by friend army— . . The effect on the men is steadily descending to that of hopelessness—People are piled all over in dingy rooms—the bunks are wooden—the buildings are grey—decrepit—guys peer from windows— some dangle leg—LATEST BATTLE CRY: "48-49-50, SOMSHIT"—Facilities are crowded all day—the chow is limited—the demand is great—The civilians dodder about in grimy clothes—the whole jumbled up community is crawling with age—the walls of blasted buildings still sag—
    Even the church windows sparkle irregularly as sun beams find broken glass—only the orange-red poppy fields seem fresh; yet the weeds and decay are choking them too—We are right in the town of Chartres—seems to be a fort or prison area—G.I.s flounder all over the place—loud speakers squawk too low to hear anything important—no hot water on the post—shower is two blocks away—How long here—what next? This place is run by German P.O.W.s—Krauts wear G.I. clothing, except for woolen, long visored caps and in some cases the German black leather belt—every chow I expect to get a

free vial of potassium cyanide—saw trainload of S.S. men yest—all staring
—weatherbeaten—AAAGH .. Maybe I should drink, swear, shoot craps
continuously—maybe I should include "fuck" between every other word—
maybe I should roll out of cafes with fleabitten whores—maybe I should
steam body to body in a hazy circle of crap shooters—But Morton doesn't—
maybe his isolation until graduation ironed something in him—wheather
good or bad I stick to my policy—the fact is I couldnt be swerved into one of
the typical anyway—I gotta have air—I know I can find Ellicotts and people
like 'm and enjoy a bond of companionship—in short at the moment I am
ETO happy—I am glad you are you and where you are—Tear this op

June 30, 1945

CHERBOURG

Cavendish—

Millions of us are going crazy waiting around—You can't say "Well we've
waited this long—be patient"—because only the moment is important—and
our moments are nothing but headaches and longing—We are located atop a
hill where we can get a splendid view of the glittering city and harbor—just as
at Edinburgh. It gives me a pang of remorse when I stand on a "boulevard"
and watch boats steam in and out—Someday I'll be able to look back at this
wasted time and sigh with relief—But if "someday" doesnt come pretty
soon I'll be a babbling idiot—

July 3, 1945

NORMANDY PENINSULA
OUTSIDE BARENTIN

Pflatti—

Germans prepare the meals and do the work—A stockade full is across the
road—our work is boring and distasteful—6 hours of guard—24 hours free
with no place to go—This aft I am standing up in a tower—with a searchlight,
stove and phone—the wind is whistling in—I am stamping on the floor and
feel the structure quiver—I sit on a box—The PWS squint up at me—I stare
back—I am beginning to wonder if maybe the individual Nazi soldier hasn't
won the war after all—The men under guard live in a hobo-town maze of
cozy cubby-holes—The interiors are brightly decorated with yellow and

maroon furniture—curtains are in the tiny windows—They stroll around tanned and healthy in G.I. clothes—O.D. blankets hang on lines—Once in a while a few men are marched out to do a short job—the others read magazines, talk, smoke—play a modified "basket-ball-soccer"—But the reason these men are so content is greater: soon they're going home—take the barbed wire fence away and they wouldnt budge—

[undated postcard]

Fraternization here is unpreventable—I see G.I.s bargaining with the heimies—giving 'em cigarettes etc—one cleaned up in hyar yest—wouldnt let us touch a thing—he is moving everything and straightening everything—he is swearing American cuss words in the heat—It's a sad state G.I.s respect the Germans as soldiers—they like their cooks—they like their work—The contrast between the sturdy Germans and the miserable French sort of hypnotizes the gullible American—he hates the "Jigs"—he hates the "Frogs"—he hates the "Limeys" but I never hear him say anything against the Jerry—Send me home. I give up—

July 15, 1945

V-Mail

I'm sitting in a bamboo easy chair on the edge of a turtle-shaped pond. Frogs are popping in the lillies, wiggling the shimmery reflections in the brown mirror surface. In my room the boys are making the poor player piano sweat. It is a New York model of birds-eye walnut, slightly dusty, creaky and out-of-tune, but nevertheless an unending source of entertainment—"Argentina Tango," "Alexander's Ragtime band," and "Beautiful Lady" come banging and wheezing out. But here's the payoff: former field Marshal Erwin Rommel used to tinkle these keys when he resided here some eighteen months ago!

July 15, 1945

Barentin—France

Gollop—

I am in the grand ball room. A player piano of birds-eye walnut rests on the powder pink carpet across the way—The walls are clothed in pale pink and gold polka dots, not extravagant at all when you look at the doo-dad studded chandelier, a writhing mass of snakes, torches, candlesticks, gargoyles and plastic swords, and the marble-mantled fireplace topped by a spotless mirror — The two large windows are thrown open and in the summer morn is a pastel blending of fluttery oaks, a quivering pool with lush pink flowers, and even a pleasing view of murky blue sky, shadowed green hillsides and petite white houses . . . Only two of us are in this room — Upstairs and around the GIS are sprawled on their cots lifeless as their towels, messkits, helmets, duffle bags and carbines which conflict with the soothing orderliness of the chateau.

This is just another stopping point along the way — We eat at another chateau several miles away — Our stockade is just as far in another direction — Our trucks are going to be running all the time, shuttling us from stockade to here to chow to hyar and thar — Le Havre isnt too far and Rouen is closer yet — Barentin is a better-class northern city untouched by the war except for a tremendous brick railroad span which is severely damaged — We'll prob'ly have to stay in tents down by the stockade to eliminate all the truck riding back and forth — Right now the jerries live in the pyramidals and are enjoying more freedoms than ever — Four guards will be on at all times and the chasers will operate in the daytime — As they say in French (not spell) com see com saw!

The ride up took about 6½ hours — Right off the bat our convoy is held up as we smell smoke and the battery is ablaze — we throw dirt on and smother it — Our truck has no fire extinguisher, no knob on the gear shift, no key, no rear view mirror — The truck behind had no brakes, no horn — every time we shifted it sounded like somone scratching his fingers on a blackboard. Ahead of us was a whole truck of krauts — quite an attraction for Bastille Day gatherings — Flags were everywhere and frenzied mobs of people — Naturally we had beaucoup difficulty in getting by and lost our convoy about ten times — In some places the people jeered, howled and threw things at the Nazis — in some places they waved to them — 457 different uniforms were noticeable, bottles were clanging all over the road and so were people who guzzled their contents. We were held up by the Seine River, which we navigated in a ferry, while the pilot was slouched in a cafe sobbing over a glass of Byrrh.

Clusters of people were along the banks swaying in the heat waves, bobbing in boats — I could hardly keep my eyes open while riding, as the hot exhaust kept coming up thru the holes in the floorboard — We were in pretty country mainly because the battered areas of Bayeaux and Caen were far behind . . . We answered the "V" waves of the kids — Picnicers [sic] dozed at roadsides, oblivious of our dust and our efforts to behead them—Settled in the chateau, tired and sweaty we sat in the gloom—Bullman is at the piano. It wheezes and bangs as he pumps but it is a cheery climax non?

July 20

Zogumph . . . [father]

Up in the chateau nook—the stupid goatlings are maaing on the lawn—way off to the right is a crummy carnival—cheveaux, gypsies and their urchin families—the kids is swarming about. They know good English (or should I say obscene American?) The PWS have perked up considerably with so much passerby attention—they sun in nothing but underpants—shout lustily while playing chess—ah yes—I am obtaining a hand made chess set from a Jerry—the German army has made these men uncanny: they rush to serve you—they wont let you heat shaving water or wash your mess kit—it is annoying to those of us who are used to doing things for ourselves—

[undated]

[Barentin]

The carnival wasn't quite rounded out—all the exhibits weren't completed—on an empty platform we deposited our wriggling terrier, "Brownie"—we needed someone who could fling fluent French so we hailed an Irishman from Boston—right off a listless crowd gathered in anticipation of G.I. doings—Brilliant McKendry began snatching up 10F notes—a bushel was collecting and we thought it was time for performing—our star was "singing" Brownie—The howls of Bullman, Brownie and I pierced the hearts of the assemblage and before long the entire crowd was around us, leaving the carnival in the cold—Just then the irate gypsy management exploded into our presence and proceeded to tell us where we could get off—

July 22

Barentin
Sunday: A day off (supposedly)

Papa asked about my physical condition—my scars are slowly turning white—My right arm is not as supple or limber as my left (it needs scientific exercise)—the area below the shoulder is still numb—I can prick it without feeling anything—my back only bothers me with extreme exercise—it tingles and itches in heat & cold—my chest is never sore—but night air has a tendency to make me cough—accordingly I refuse to pull night guard (and dont)—it will take another six months for the adhesion in my back to clear up (your observations are correct—there are thousands of guys with discharges running around in better condition than me)—But I am not alone over here —guys getting out on points are those with <u>long</u> service—not men with decorations and wounds—I am now in a category 4 outfit—meaning it is to be inactivated upon return—[meanwhile] I am learning French and German —met a hawk eyed Nazi from the 11th Panzer (the guys that made me wot I am today) He is useful as an instructor—since he speaks English (Oxford and New York accents)—The huns are having the time of their lives—M.P.s had to fire their weapons last nite to keep people away from and out of the cage—

July 29, 1945

BARENTIN—FROGLAND

Tragna—

Las nite I watch our boys play Germans in soccer game—This is German national pastime, and they are butting the ball with their heads, elbows and rumps and are scrambling strenuously without stopping—The men on the sidelines are screaming and it sounds like a world series—Strangely enough they only beat us 5-3—Nite befo we play them in football—but they can understand it not a little—is mostly passing with "touch" football and to them is great foolishness—

The guards are in the cage more time than out—reason being there is nothing else to do than fraternize with Nazis—which they do to the limit— they go to great lengths to give them cigarettes—thus antagonizing the passing French, the idea in a nutshell—it seems that hostility on the part of certain French has seeped into the American minds—They are gradually being seduced by the Germans—whose good looks, good nature and intelligence stand out in contrast to the French—so here goes the old snowball again—by the time we leave Europe we'll love the Germans and loathe everyone else . . .

Most of the prisoners (we have no "S.S." men) seem utterly without sense of guilt—they believe what they were doing was necessary and wonder why we came over here in the first place—yesterday went out again to Camp "Old Gold" to straighten wire installments—Before long we were talking to the noncoms—a French boy scout passed with a knife in a sheath arousing comment—like Hitler Jugund the German said—then he tells us there was

no Hitler youth before 1933—he says that's when he first suspected Germany was preparing for war—he comes in the army in 1938—in the airforce—He is a prisoner of war for one year—is bitter—has not heard from home in over a year—one thing leads to another—I show him "Time" magazine telling of last days of Berlin—He calls it propaganda—he is very surprized to hear of Russian occupation—We tell him how "the big three" gets along in Germany —We discuss sports—"Basketball is for women"—

They are very amiable on all subjects but war—When we sum up (experimenting) by telling him our purpose of occupation—education etc.— to build up Germany and its industry to make them understand that they benefit more without weapons—he stands looking at us with his head back, half smirking—like a small boy being tongue-lashed for a wrong—knowing he could have got away with it if he'd not made so many mistakes—it is true that the Germans are one of the cleanest—farthest advanced people in Europe but flushing their minds is a hopeless task—only solution I can see is occupation for 50 years—

August 5

BARENTIN

Our leader, the sex-fiend Sergeant Walter, presently arrived, writhed his blood-red lips, twitched his nose, sucked in his cheeks, upped and downed his eyebrows alternately, squinted his heartless brown eyes, ruffled his black, silky hair and stunned us with a melodramatic bellow—He is the super-egoist, a sadist, and another genius. His specialty is lycanthropism, thru which he has acquired a horde of females, merely to satisfy his needs, which to him are as important as eating or sleeping—Walter isn't a large man, but he has a powerful look and a powerful voice. He has a hairless chest, a woman's vanity when it comes to fingernails and the lust of a beast when it comes to women —With savage dashes of fluent French or German he explains to me that he is hoping to attend the University of Chicago, to be thrust upon the waiting world as a master of voice, drama, journalism, art and music—Much as he is hated and feared and discussed (He wears a helmet liner, luger, bayonet, German belt and raincoat into town) by his men, Walter has a personality all his own, that commands for him the respect of a celebrity—

Those thoughts aren't exactly those of McKendry—A shaggy black head burrows out from white wrinkled sheets, a bleary blue eye pops open and blinks in cadence with his mouth: "One hiccough," he croaks, "one hiccough from me, and the wretch Walter will grovel at me feet!"

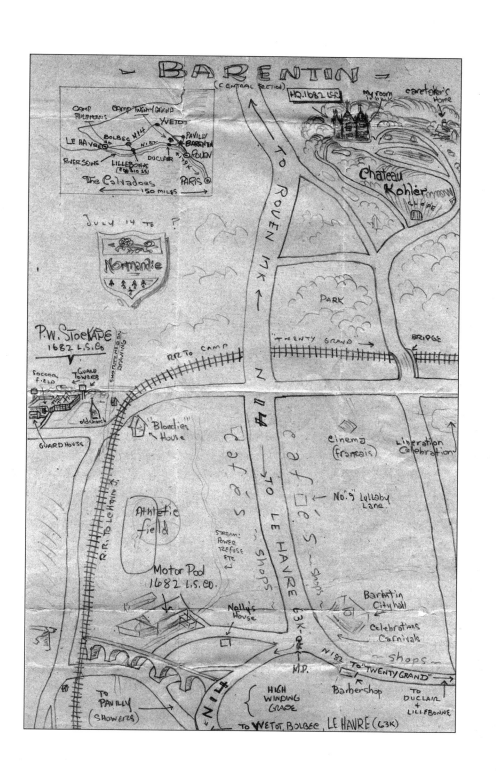

BARENTIN

(CENTRAL SECTION)

HQ. 1682 L.S.Co.

my room in back

caretaker's Home

Camp Philippeaus

Camp Twenty Grand

YVETOT

Bolbec N/14

N.152

PAVILLY

BARENTIN

LE HAVRE

DUCLAIR

ROUEN

RIVER SEINE

LILLEBONNE

(80 & 810 SS)

PARIS

The Calvados

150 MILES

JULY 14 TO ?

Normandie

TO ROUEN N14

Chateau Kohler

CHAPEL

P.W. STOCKADE

1682 L.S. Co.

PARK

Soccer field

GUARD TOWER

TWENTY GRAND

BRIDGE

RR TO CAMP

SEE ROUTE HERE ON DRAWING

N #14

GUARD HOUSE

old church

Blondie's House

TO LE HAVRE

cinema (Francais)

Liberation Celebration

cafés ~ shops

No."s Lullaby Lane

R.R. TO LE Havre &

Athletic field

STREAM: POWER GARBAGE ETC.

Motor Pool 1682 L.S. Co.

cafés ~ Shops

Barentin City hall

Celebrations Carnivals

shops

Nelly's House

N #14

M.P.

N152 TO "TWENTY GRAND"

TO PAVILLY (SHOWERS)

HIGH WINDING GRADE

Barbershop

TO DUCLAIR + LILLEBONNE

TO YVETOT, BOLBEC, LE HAVRE (63K)

63K 24-

August 7

BARENTIN

Odzig:

Another pleasant day — The doglets are gloofling about. The newest member, a brown & white squeaker, has accompanied his master to the motor pool — that was my job yesterday — Nothing last nite in town — McK was thoroughly mauled by some Frenchmen in an alley — so he stayed upon his bed, whimsically casting about his profound observations — we listened to Bing Crosby sing "An Irish Lullaby" (on the phonograph) — gabbed about everything and the old madhouse was flourishing — Corrigan, another Irishman joined us — and before long was again relating his trip to the green isle — "If you ever want to restore your faith in human nature," he says, "go to Ireland" — Soon I am experiencing my first taste of whisky — some "White Horse" scotch that Corrigan gets in non coms rations — I have it with coke — nothing but a prolonged burning in my stomach — the one drink does not light me up — but it keeps me alert longer so that I am able to enjoy the cultural conversation —

. . . we waver under the light faces practically pressed together — it finally gets around to "the Jew" (I am the same nationality as Corrigan's wife — Lithuanian!!) I am encouraged to hear McKendry announce that he sees hope for the Jew-boy — "They're mingling," he says — "They feel at home with us . . getting away from their persecution complex — their mannerisms — it will all work out — but he says — I have no particular attraction to the black man — we shut him up by telling him certain Ethiopians and hindus are of the white race — I'll never forget a story an <u>officer</u> told a large class on orientation at the 19th repo — An old Jew was standing in the doorway of his pawn shop. A drunk staggered by — "You're a goddam Jew" said the drunk. "You're a goddam drunk" said the Jew — The drunk laughed and laughed — "Yeah but tomorrow I'll be sober and you'll still be a G.D.J.!" <u>Nobody</u> <u>laughed.</u>

McKendry is always dreaming of the island paradise on which he can "really live" — but then he thinks of the flat he had on 225th St N.Y. He was continually ordering up stuff and throwing the containers out the window — He used to wander near the river by Columbia University, seeing men in boiled white shirts, women with yowling babies on their breasts — and he liked it — in all the turmoil of the big city, he was alone — I tell him of Duluth — "Oh, you of the provinces" he dismisses me with a haughty inflection and wave —

McK is the only person I've ever found that can use F--- as an adjective and make it sound funny—We are still hounding the egotistic, oversexed Walter—This morning I draw a picture of him naked, clutching a dress, drooling over a bed—I show it to a psycho's psycho—guy named Piazza —"Is he taking a bath?" he says . .

For some reason this letter strikes me as unnecessarily vulgar—but you've got to understand the unbounded enjoyment I derive from these characters— Not that I hold myself apart—Morton, in spite of all he has encountered is still undeveloped along certain lines—whether it can be remedied remains to be seen—We got our Eisenhower jackets today—to some it's an indication of homeward passage—but to me it's just another blow in the face—This satire can never end—

August 11, 1945

Barentin

Proapus

'ad rather an interesting day . . we thundered by a huge box factory and entered busy Bolbec, as charming a town as you'd expect for northern France—From there I transferred to a converted ambulance and rolled into Lillebonne—I was opposite the 810th mess hall, a hotel restaurant devoted to GIS exclusively—I watched a Frenchman decorate a lavish cake, then caught a ride to headquarters—within 15 minutes my mission was completed—I saw my service record, a typewriter was pounding out a letter, which was signed by the CO—requesting that I be given another physical. So far so good. The next step is the actual examination.* . . I was happy for some of my colleagues, including the unsurpassable Sgt Walter who were given the green light sign for a journey home—Nervous wrecks, they frothed into trucks and tearfully whimpered adieu. No good rumors were available, only "ifs"—Tonite we wait for Japan's reaction to the emperor under our commander's offer

---

*I hoped a slight Butzdorf wound, on my knee, would get me more departure points.

August 12

Barentin

Osan:

This moment, one year ago, we were gliding up the Clyde in the splendid, white "Lizzy" — I'd see the hills even greener than they were if I was where you are — .. McKendry slouches back on his bed, his eyebrow nervously twitching, as he watched a fly crawl over his knee — "Wouldnt you love to be a bear" he hacks — "Drowzing on the grassy slopes of the Rocky mountains, the insects colliding against your furry face — crunch, crunch, crunch — Suddenly you are aware of the warm, earthy smell of an elk — saliva gushes into your mouth and over your pink tongue — what tasty-looking bastards! eat, eat, eat, eat MANGER!!" McKendry rises, lurches toward me, eyes and teeth gleaming. He halts, squinting: "Betrayed" he screams, "you're only a baboon!"

August 13

Boozla:

Today we had big chocolate-coated cherry sponge cake for "vj" Day but no announcement is made yet so we keep having cake, day after day, until it is the day — Our former fuhrer [Sgt] Walter has left for de u.s. McKendry will undoubtedly take over the spotlights — His latest exploits are most unusual — He selects a house, walks up to it, turns doorknob, walks in, settles himself in the most comfortable chair and begins an amiable cognac-coated chat with the stunned people — if they do not react favorably, as no one in such a situation would, he becomes en-raged — "pigs! — swine!" — he roars and staggers out to try another habitat — "The greatest opportunity of mankind today," he gurgles, "is to follow in the foamy wake of the most phenomenal intellectual sage of the era — none other than my humble self!"

August 16, 1945

Barentin — France

VJ Day

We didnt hit our sacks until early this morning — was nothing extravagant — just a smokey gabfest with beer gulping and clamouring radio — I led bands, I beat drums, I swayed in sympathy with glazed, bloodshot eyes that blinked

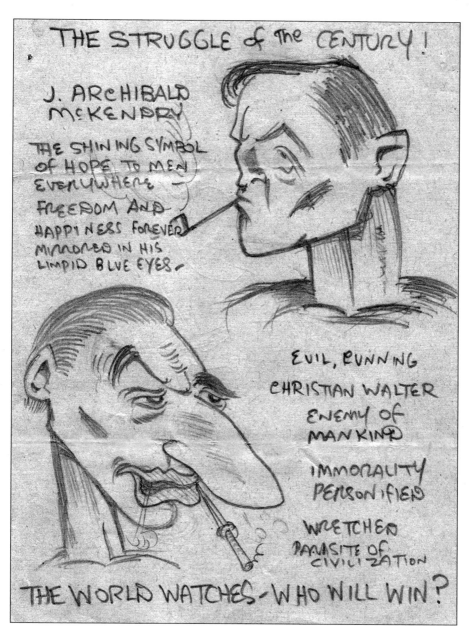

In the lulling routine of Barentin, my imagination took over, inventing comic book titans—transforming troublesome Mac and caricaturing with mischief, not rancor, our remarkable sergeant.

and swam in their sockets like prunes in boiling water—McKendry bored his face into our exuberance—He'd somehow groped his way downtown, had heard music, talk, seen bright lights, wandered in. It was a wedding—An empty chair was conveniently placed at the head of the table, and it was appropriately occupied—McKendry soon received several sharp hints to vacate—with a magnificent gesture he swept off his cap, pushed back his chair, and heaved himself to his feet—the tension was mounting.

Then began the most sensational awe-inspiring utterance that ever soothed the ears of the peasants—a flare of color in their drab existence—McKendry worked himself up to a peak of emotion, concluding with "My father was here, and now I am here, so that France may be free!"

With tears in his eyes he sank back on a wave of thunderous applause and shaking floor-boards—He was the white-haired boy. "Yes," he says "It will forever be engraved on the alabaster walls of my memory"—

No other incidents except the horn got stuck as we sped to a shower—as people poured out of the houses we responded with arms out-stretched above our heads—the Eisenhower "V"—...Somebody says the war's over—I say "Everywhere but France!"—

August 17

McKendry lurked in the shadows last nite, articulate enough to be objectionable—He attempted to batter the kitchen door down, but his hunger soon gave way to stunned amuzement, and he laughed himself horizontal.

Another "Mac"

This Mac is keeping up my morale here—he's the Irishman from Boston whose father was a thief and his mother a scrub woman in an office building—This Mac is a "cha-rac-tuh"—He is loose-jointed .. with large extremities—He lost a finger tip and suffered a broken nose and a speech deficiency in an automobile accident—His face of sharp hollows and dreary blue eyes framed by gable ears is a masterpiece of malformation—but his voice, mannerisms and vocabulary top anything I've yet encountered—He speaks in a halting but intense rasp that squeezes past his bobbing cigarette to astound and entrance you—

Mac is one of those happy-go-lucky, heavy drinking, take-what-comes guys that keep everybody happy—every word, every action is a gem—His knowledge of the English and French vocabulary is uncanny .. He can quote from any poetry and knows the philosophy of the ages—His glossary of technical terms is complete—and evidently he has dabbled in all the arts and sciences—

Mac was one of the rear echelon guys who slept between sheets in Rennes for 9 months while I was in my foxhole—He has been into the bowels of France just as he has seen the slum life of America—He is at home in filth or cleanness—drinking to him is a delightful pastime—He'd rather live 20 years his way than "60 years" my way—

When Mac is serious you're quivering with delight—His dry sardonic humor—even when unintentional—is a revelation—He has that certain amount of insanity that clicks with me—He is a gigantic key and unlocks himself—Every thought is a parody on living—He is a walking satire of all things good and a talking personification of all things bad—His imagination is never throttled—ten times last night he flashes me a silencing glance—stares off into the scores of spider webs in the corner and croaks:—"This huge brute of a man, red faced—and blustery burst into my magnificent mansion atop a wind-swept hill, threw his gleaming oilskins in a heap and crashed over to the fireplace—'Gad WHAT A NIGHT,' he roared—'Certainly—I've been expecting you—won't you sit down for a cup of tea?'"

This makes as much sense as our usual topics—when this cha-rac-tuh isn't lecturing us or pouring out his rath—we listen while he convinces innocent people that the MPs are after them or "Somebody wants them downstairs"—He has a certain gift of the dramatic and a deep understanding of human nature that classifies him above a practical joker—Believe it or not he can be as serious as death if he wants to be—if he were to see what I have written here—he would turn upon me with a wrinkled brow—his blue eyes would flash and his jaw snap with his fingers and he'd snarl: "Son, if you ever—uh—approach this lofty pedestal on which I've surveyed—uh—civilization the past—uh—23 years, you would realize that—uh—clearness and conciseness are—uh—desired—This childish prattle is—uh—superfluous and—uh—entirely unnecessary .. Simply tell them I am a genius!"—

ANOTHER "JERRY"

The German that was with us today speaks very fluent English—As a former student he understands philosophy and literature and is a very definite anti-Nazi in the political aspect—He lives near the German-Holland border and before his conscription into the German army in 1941 he was a student at a university in Hamburg—All he wants now is solitude where he can do a bit of writing and devote his life to his god—"Beauty"—

"Four eyes" deserted from the German army last August, even though he had a comparatively "soft" job in Paris—dressed as a civilian he attempted to flee over the Swiss border but was apprehended by French communists who treated him very well—He has been in our custody for ten months—He can't understand "why men with his principles are not being sent back to Germany to spread Democratic ideas"—He can't see why there is so much hate for the Germans in Europe—"The people didn't want war," he states—"but by the time the Nazis got control it was too late to do much about it"—

In most stockades about 70% of the Germans are on the fence—ready to swing with the "strongest nation"—only about 5% are anti-Nazis and the rest are dyed-in-the-wool Nazis—Gradually he says some of the 70% will be won over—But the rest will still retain their old ideas—He believes in a vast educational program—But fails to see how it can be accomplished when communistic and democratic countries are working together—Once the democratic ideas can succeed—he will never trust a dictator—If Hitler were in Moscow and Stalin in Berlin <u>we</u> <u>would</u> <u>have</u> <u>attacked</u> <u>Stalin</u>—The average German has no guilt—He believes Poland started all the trouble, after which Britain and France declared war on Germany—The German is a great believer in secret weapons—He justifies the V-bombing of London as a revenge for the British bombing of Germany.

"4 eyes" first contact with Americanism was several "Newsweek" magazines he found in Paris (although he had American instructors in Hamburg). He is rather disappointed in "Life" because it seems too sensational—When the German occupation is lifted a German from East Germany (Russia) will not recognize one under American occupation—People in great multitudes act as beasts—first they want bread—then they want freedom—They are in the "bread stage" now—I wish they would let me write to my family—It is right that Germany should furnish labor as reparation to countries that were destroyed—I am willing to work but not as a prisoner of war—An Italian philosopher has a dangerous theory—"Attack your neighbor if you are strong for you may not be strong again"—A German philosopher said "Every man must be a hero—if he is not a hero he is a coward"—

"Four eyes" is 23 years old—Another unusual character—I shall speak more with he . . .

August 26, 1945

Hi Strung!

Leave us seh-chle this onct and for all: — First off I is oilin mah shootin arn in readiness for that ornery sawd-off-skonk: Zeke Davis — Jest another bit of proof thet all air corpse men is a mite teched — 'course mebbe 'twant all his fault — I told him my physical condition as we sat on top story of a bus speeding between Coventry and Birmingham — it was hot — dusty — noisy — and women were attractively scratching — so he prob'ly wasnt paying much attention to me — even if he did bid me adieu with the mistaken impression that I was a miserable wreck — he should never convey such ideas to you, my humble mother. — I strongly recommend that he be struck upon his proboscis, outstanding as it is, and that you be severely chastised for your thoughtless rush to bad conclusions —

Here, again, my case history: On Jan 27 near Sinz, Germany I was struck by shrapnel, which lacerated my pleura, lung and lodged in the diaphram — in order to operate successfully, a partial re-section was made of the right 7th rib. Aspiration to remove blood and air from my lung chamber was made at Thionville, and additional aspirations were made at the 160th gen'l — to return the function of the lung to normal — up to Feb 4 it was necessary to use an oxygen mask — but from then on I used both lungs unaided —

Owing to the concentrated excercise applied to the region of the right thorax for over sixty days I was able to obtain "lung control," a condition of breathing superior to that of the average person — I can now breathe out of either lung as simply as opening or closing either eye!! . .

In the strenuous moving process, I was required to exert myself abnormally, thus inducing a general weakened condition, a cough, and other internal stress — since early July, however, I have slept, eaten and lived as leisurally (?) as though I'd been in a hospital — I am far from such polluted places as Cherbourg or LeHavre — I usually feel pretty good — I am not being "kicked around from place to place" — It is true that I am as good as useless — not to the army — but in the capacity I find myself at the present — we are simply occupying our time, while waiting for the monster of an army to disband — The little wheels are turning, and sooner or later we're bound to find ourselves on top of a shipping list —

August 30, 1945

Barentin — France

Ahmunns —

McKendry — Piazza — and I went for an after-supper stroll — Passed thru a labyrinth of trees and mushrooms — overlooking the Le Havre bound railroad tracks — We wandered up into the apple orchards — plucking healthy fruit as we went — in the lanes the trees were unbelievably tall and frosty green — We picked our way thru speckled shadows and humming foliage, leading to a subdued and quiet intersection in the middle of the wood — Eight lanes branched off into the gloom, and beside them was twisted metal and holes — The trees were hacked with names like Randy, Raymond, showing that we were in a former bivouac area of the R.A.F.

(Above and opposite) As a change from slapdash sketches and cartoons, I tried highly stylized drawings, in pencil on brown paper, of the local French and the GI presence. More contact with French citizens is the subject of the August 30 letter.

We inspected peaches, peas, grapes and lofty poplars with rustic houses reposing at their feet. Down the slope we went, crossing the tracks, a road, perspiring in scented air—"See if we can get into the park"—McKendry says —We see a glowing stretch of lawn—smooth as a golf course—lined with trim, dense shrubbery, a rainbow stream of soft-hued flowers, glistening pools floating white flowers and the images of fragile trees—White walks traveled out to all extremes, gently merging into greenness and sunlight—in silence we walked thru the gate, saw we were in somebody's front yard!—Far off to the right was a yellow and rust colored chateau—it rose, clean and simple, sturdy and modern, a symbol of the beauty of its land—a gigantic dog kennel was beneath a muff of forestry—sleek animals pressed their noses to the bars and whimpered—white sheep pulled against their chains and trampled the grass as our outlines caught their eye—A clean, laughing little boy in a blue suit came running out to meet us—an older boy, sitting on wide steps, rose and joined the younger—The party was completed by a minute girl-child with intense blue eyes and clean hair and rosy cheeks—we are amazed no little— McKendry is very gruff—He introduces himself coldly, and offers the older boy a cigarette—Piazza runs his fingers along the smaller boy's face—

I keep looking at the landscape—within fifteen minutes we are all seated on a wide verandah—under a red umbrella—wine is hissing before us—and two lively-looking females are speaking to us in cultured English—They laugh easily and touch their lips to American cigarettes, which they offer to us (the cigarettes). Egad—what is going on?—is this the ravaged, beaten, poverty-stricken people of France? We are so surprized we don't even worry about the sloppy fatigue clothes we have on—The girls are flushed and radiant in thin yellow slacks—It seems their father made all his money on the toilet paper factory in town—naturally there isn't much of a market for the stuff in France—but he perfumes his paper and it comes in handy for wiping greasy faces—

We would have lounged around for hours—but an American Ford breezes up, containing some very tall, neatly dressed young men—They are brushing the gooey hair out of their eyes and are looking at us with abject horror—"Bonswar" we say and limply grab eight or nine wrists—

We swagger down the walk—A lumpy sheep bolts before us—McKendry closes one eye and glares at the sheep. The sheep, terrified, strains on its chain, bulges its eyes, twitches its velvety lips—McKendry bends down in a grotesque arc—"You son-of-a-bitch!" he says—Two dozen incredulous eyes usher us out the gate. . . .

Barentin

September 2

Dept of Understatement

Duluth, Minn. Aug. 15, 1945

Dear Mort:—You may have heard that the Japs surrendered!—

[Father]

September 6

Hocp:

Dance tonite—pws baked rolls and cake all last nite—A wild-eyed woman was operating upstairs—but she was only in our room ten minutes—I opened the windows

September 11

Gorzaz

Got a bit of a surprize this evening . . QM 290 sent me a little package of my personal belongings salvaged from Germany, including the original Butzdorf story and my last letter home—although seven months have passed since I've seen all this, it seemed as if I'd had them all the time, they were so familiar—

September 18
V-Mail

[to mother]

The niece of the Swiss lady wot owns this place is vacationing here—our Lt is riding her around—Dont know if the peoples is looking at her with jealousy or scorn—

Mort

September 23

Sunday

Moafa:

I talk with Francis Xavior Corrigan — who is professor at Princeton — he is living on Lungeyeland, New York — He is marrying a girl name o' Kate — which he is knowing all his life, as she lives just around the corner . . He is now writing a book on "Elementary Algebra"!

September 26

Gormk:

Going down to Lillebonne — we enter the gate — who steps out of the guardhouse — attired in white helmet and yellow armband but — the one and only Archibald McK! — He now works 7 hours every two days — spends his other hours reading Keats — touring the German-loving countryside — Mac was completing a letter to his brother — but decided to kindle a fire — "It did not convey the mood I intended" —

I hope you is at school where you should be — Big disappointment if you not — By the by — when David had the car why didn't you see if you could find this Barbara?

September 27–30, 1945 (a paraphrase-reminiscence) — Five of us truck to Paris — "a glorious rat-race for us" but "Europe's greatest attraction" (I avowed in another race — for superlatives). True, we covered it all — the Eiffel Tower, the Metro, the Louvre, the Sorbonne, the cafes, the five thousand 94th "boys" in town, and inevitably the Folies Bergère and its "Paris Cocktail": "devils crack whips over women who have sinned, buffoons frolic, princes climb rope ladders to castle windows grasping white roses and swords. The orchestra wildly gnashes its piece in the pits." We "tag along" to Pigalle, "sit in various smokey places, unmoved by the pent-up ferocious music, usually rendered on but a fiddle or accordian. The piano player looks at you" — he's there too — "eyes glazed. He smiles horribly in the bright light, and plunges to his dirge on the keys." Later, "wild-eyed women are not inviting looking, just inviting." But for us it's "machine kaput." On the last day, the Arc de Triomphe soon grows smaller and smaller, and it is not reassuring to feel the "grasp of the army" once more. But it's good to think "je reviende. I can always come back."

October 13, 1945

Barentin

V-Mail

Oapm:

Frosty Morning—Frostier—no mail! Got a job near Rouen—Took the pws—
out in a cow pasture to pick up wire and poles from a farmer's land—They
spend most of the time gorging themselves in an apple orchard—German pws
under the French came up—they had worn out, dirty clothes, practically no
shoes—looked with envy—at our well-fed contented ones—

October 14, 1945

Barentin

oopa

Big batch mail come in yesterday—and I am churned up all over—first I
read in "Stars & Stripes" that the whole redeployment system is snafued—
withdrawal of Queen Lizzy—Acquitania—etc—strikes—no ships—storms—
  I am as stationary here as the front door—everyone pushes me back and
forth—but I stay in one place—
  Two letters arrive from Co A 376 inf. They contain evidence making me
eligible for oak leaf cluster for purple heart—In other words I will be eligible
for discharge—But the trouble is—I have to wait until all the 80s, 70s and 63s
go home—you never read about it in the paper—but there are still 100
pointers here . . A guy in this outfit has 125 points but they wont let him go
home because he's supposed to be dead! we have the biggest navy in the
world—where is it?
  . . . Been busy going out on a wire job—A farmer wanted dead wire and
poles removed from his property near Rouen. So we tramp around with p.w.s
in apple orchards, cow pastures, sugar beets, woods, and fields—we get chased
by horses—cows—and sheep—hard to walk without slithering on apples—
scrunch scrunch scrunch—Here the French are supposed to be starving—and
they let their apples rot on the ground so they can make cider later on—The
orchards were stinking slightly—the Germans stuffed themselves with the
ripe fruit—I don't care for them too much—not quite as sweet as those in

Brittany — The big Germans grab the poles in one hand — shake 'em — pull 'em out — throw 'em over a shoulder and walk away —

After I took my papers up to the hospital in Rouen I had a haircut by a G.I. barber — first time since May — good old electric shears again —

October 14, 1945

BARENTIN

Talked with Corrigan — He is our 1st Sgt now — Grad — of St. John's — instructor — math, hist., english Princeton U. — for a test question I say — "How would you like it if you had a younger brother three years ahead of you in school, practically a genius when you come home?" — He is telling me that I know things "he'll" never know — that I have it all first hand — and I say so what — it's only an interpretation of values — the majority of cases are content with book larnin — as long as they don't have to suffer to obtain the information — and he is telling me that "I am young now — and that what happened had to be — and I am endowed with enough intelligence to benefit and appreciate what I <u>did</u> get out of it all — and later on I will realize it" — and I say so what again — a man's life is what he wants it to be — naturally he accepts — forceably or otherwise what falls in his path — but at the same time it's an individual's world — my brother is just as well off — or even better — in <u>his</u> world — as I am, having wasted two years — where I would have been away from home <u>anyway</u> — (in college) and having the handicap of a physical ailment hung on me for life — so we end in a stalemate —

October 15

BARENTIN

Aps—

Just got back from Lillebonne—watched 'em change my score to 62 points—
This point deal was quite a struggle—I landed in the 810th with 37 points
—and with perseverance have pushed it up to 62—They started calling
me "Round trip" running down to Lillebonne all the time—Finally brought
results but the outcome is questionable—New redeployment snafu has delayed
everyone's homecoming—I managed to accumulate 62 points thusly:

24 months of service—	24
13 mos overseas	13
Battle Star "Northern Fr"	5
"Ardennes"	5
"Rhineland"	5
Purple Heart	5
Oak Leaf Cluster	5
	62

Today guys with 70 points or more were removed from shipping lists—so
you see where I stand—some of they is getting dangerously drunk and is
threatening to become communists etc—morale is at a new low—"Why
doesn't our 'big' navy take us back?" Meanwhile I try to take my mind off
things—New AFN station here makes for good reception—Leading song is
"Stardust"—"Laura" has caught on and is undoubtedly best of recent songs—
also Vaughn Monroe's "There I've said it Again"—

On October 16 we left Barentin to deliver an eighty-one-pointer to a homeward-
bound outfit in Liège, Belgium. It was to be a six hundred–mile motor trip
—extravagant? I didn't ask: there was a vast supply of idle men and trucks—"I
rode in style: borrowed a lawn chair from Corrigan—padded it with a sleeping
bag—wedged it with the 81 pointer's bags. [. . .] We rode through a steady
archway of trees" past wagons packed with sugar beets—"Hit Amiens around
lunch time and gassed up." All you do is sign a slip and take off. "Nearing the

'Bulge' territory," we began to see "little white crosses and shell holes" but also much industrial activity. "Electric street cars always ran in chains of three or more clogging the whole street." There were American cars and signs in English: "Week-End Hotel," "Come-On-In Tavern." We deliver our man to a "huge" warehouse bin in Liège, where others wait lethargically to leave for the States. The MPS are German PWs! Near the German border, along with the heavy industry we see piles of coal and smoking conversion plants. "but the Meuse river runs on serene and shining." We were impressed with the Belgians, who, it seems, "are quicker to patch up than the French."*

October 21

Moazn:

. . . I dream of sitting in your room smoking an Arabian water pipe—I greet you with a gesture—"Sit down" I say—"I'll be with you in a minute"—PWs making me nice suitcase—box—

*Due to its length, I paraphrased parts of this letter.

October 24

Foosa:

—Just got orders to depart for the Riviera—a "seven day furlough"—Had the pws make me a fancy-like suitcase and camera case—We head for Lillebonne tomorrow morning—was down thar yesterday—picked up twelve pws at the big central enclosure 23 (50,000 [prisoners of war]) outside of Bolbec—The members of the guard and administration really live soft—claim to have the best chow in the ETO—'Twas good—had big hot buns—They still get plenty loot and watches from pws—All ova' the place is built up miniature cities— castles—forts—statue of liberties—maps of u.s.—decorations worked out in stones and flowers—The stockade is tremendous—pws huddle around, like sheep—Big job—taking care o' 'em—

October 25, 1945

LILLEBONNE

Mahmin:

We jeep to LeHavre at 1930—Take a train to Paris about 2030—in Paris we have a whole day to ourselves—meet a furlough group and take off tomorrow night—Blustery day—We play with "Lil Pierre"—whose mama works here in the chateau—his papa is in a nearby pw cage—Nice set up here—They sold 4 horses to French—proceeds go for cognac!

Slong Mort

October 28, 1945

NICE, FRANCE
COTE D'AZUR

Allo from Paradise! Having wonderful time—wish I were there—This is it! We traveled 23 hours from Paris in crowded—dirty cars—stepped off into something cool & clean — Bullman loses his wallet — we get assigned to our hotel — we finally find it — not bad — but no hot water — I take loovely hot shower next door — Whole city is white, orange & yellow — with low — broad Spanish tile roofs — Fact the whole land shows Spanish influence — mission-type cathedrals — cacti-rocks and beeg palms — The Mediterranean of course is bluer than blue — we eat in hotel — are served — white tablecloths — army must pay fortune for all this —

November 6

BARENTIN

I was overcome with emotion when I received mom's lovely <u>tooth</u>picks — I'll cherish them always — and the dear little washrag! I have four now! A detailed story [of the furlough] should arrive sometime — The sun did come out the last two days and we made use of it — as soon as we reached there we were given an envelope and a hotel room — didnt take us long to freshen up — wot a place! We could walk around with no hat, no tie — buttons unbuttoned — sleeves rolled up — Every form of entertainment and amusement was free — and best of all there is more English spoken there than French — of course the whole place was built up by wealthy Americans — Jay Gould contributed $8,000,000 for a casino — (now the red cross) J.P. Morgan, Vanderbilts — have villas there — John Barrymore has a goajus one with a blue roof — The Mediterranean is 'eavenly blue — the trees too — are impressive — tall, tapering, candle-like — yews — orange trees — pink — peeling eucaliptis — feathery — maritime pine — sooty-trunked olive trees — chunky royal palms lace-like kaki (Japanese persimmon) and the frosty-leafed pepper tree cactus sprouts on the hillsides — the siege of color is all backed by the misty peaks of the maritime alps

November 7

BARENTIN

Poper:

Dont take those "complaining letters" too seriously — it's much easier to wield a melancholy pen than sit down and cry — As you know LeHavre was put off limits because of the goings-on I told you about before — now they are considering the same treatment for Rouen — worst thing is — guys come in

from Germany—They are so in love with that wonderful country that they can't stand the French and do not try to cover it up at all—Time after time I overhear conversations concerning the relative merits of the Germans and French—The "masterrace"—invariably wins—The chief trouble with the american soldier is plain ignorance—Which will undoubtedly spread when they get back—as for me—I am eligible for discharge—I am also in Europe—
HAW

Mort

November 7, 1945

BARENTIN

Brawntschic:

Raccrochez, s'il vous plait. Les montagnes sontelles hautes? Souvelez le avec soin ou pouvons-nous traverser la Riviere? Wo ist ein friseur? We ist eine toilette? Bringen sie mich zu einen lazarett. Wie hassen sie? Haw—that'll send you scurrying—Nov 14 we leave here (Barentin) for parts unknown—The 810 as usual tries to cheer us up by telling us we'll be on the water around Dec 7—Whenever a date is mentioned you know they are giving you a snow yob—mainly cause not even port authorities know when you'll sail—From Nice I send you one package—whose contents demand not only an explanation—but an excuse—

The necktie was made in Eze—one of the oldest cities in France—Which is still perched atop a tremendous rock overlooking the Mediterranee—The people live there without electricity—heat or running water because they do not have to pay taxes to the French government (maintaining historic property). In their spare time they work their grimy fingers to the marrow, making napkin rings, refrigerator handles and yes, neckties—so that foppish people like you, secure across the sea, can drape it about your silly necks—The sun rises on their chins, sets on their necks (from the perspiration they make pure scotch whiskey) and they slave for you—I met one female woman who is appealing to me moron any I've met on this side—She is being born in New York—but is living in Nice for nine years—She is a guide on Monte Carlo-Grasse tours and for some strange reason is sit beside me—I get over my fright and talk like the clever, normal chimpanzee I rally am—I like how she listen attentively while I rave about Salvatore Dali and Dick Tracy—She go to great trouble to point out a eucalyptis tree to me—(mebbe she is sorry for me cause she thinks I am koala bear) (Yes, but come to think of it—I had a haircut that morning) Any hoo—anyhoo (that's twice) I take her to show "Kind Lady"—seeing it for 2nd time—and make very dramatic goodby next morning—

'nother memory of Nice—This song "Symphony" is drive me nuts—they play it down there without stop—After I learn French words—you can play it for me while mama scratch my back— . . Now then about this "Hon" is for me to say what I address you as—after all I am giving my life's corpuscles for the right of free speech, free assembley, free dishes with every five gallons—besides "Hon." doesnt stand for what you think: it is simply an abbreviation for honnoyance!

Mort

November 8

Morska:

Spent the night at the motor pool—"Ox" woke me up with his barking— "Ox" is one of the "puppies" we brought from Isigny—Only now he's as big as a sheep dog—and is being used as a guard in the gasoline cage, mainly because (1) he was killing chickens up near the chateau—and (2) someone walked off with all the gasoline 'tuther night.—The Lt gets the bright idea someone should guard the motor pool . . . So I get him every other night—

McKendry is back—It seems Barentin is considered the Devil's Island of 810 detachments—so all undesirable characters are shipped down here—Mac decides to go to town and tries to crash out the gate with a command car. The first Sgt runs in the chateau—yelling "McKendry's gone crazy!"—thus recruiting assistance—A bunch of men drag Mac up the hill and try to stick his head under a faucet—Mac wrecks the latrine and charges after the captain —Piazza (the kid who uses white shoe polish for face lotion) hung on to the captain's waist and the three of them whirled around into insensibility—

Next morning McK is hailed into the office—now after a good drunk he always feels cheerful—full of vigor—But one look at the Captain's face and he loses his smirk—"Stay here" the captain says. "You're under arrest"—McK calmly sits down, cleans his nails with the captain's gold letter opener—The Captain comes back—looks at arrogant McK., almost bursts into tears—"I underestimated you"—he yells "And now—And now—"

Yesterday afternoon McK saunters into our orderly room—"Gentlemen" he croaks "The lamb is back!"

Mort

November 9

BARENTIN

Oakka:

'Ad a haircut yest in Rouen—later saw "Johnny Angel"—the town is off limits as you know—But the cafe owners wont let that last long—There is a general hostility toward the Americans now—mostly because of the spreading crime wave carried on by displaced persons, Poles and Frenchmen in American uniforms—naturally an American uniform means a "Yank"—minor retaliation is being carried on by the flustered French—even in Barentin— big freight cars were continually rolled up in front of the motor pool so our trucks couldn't get in. This was not a problem long—the PWS and the trucks simply pushed the cars away—angering the French who promptly pushed them back again—

This went on for a few days—Then sand and gravel was poured over the tracks, making a driveway—next time the cars came down they were derailed—The poor French sweated all day with horses getting them back on the tracks—instead of ending the incident—the cars were right back in front of the doors next day—Shaw (motor Sgt) told 'em that if they were found there again he'd pour gas on 'em and burn 'em up.—This burned up the Frenchman. He tore up to the chateau—where the problem was finally settled—

Meanwhile—other acts were going on—our water was being turned off—we found it wasn't the pump or machine—A PW was sent to put a lock on the door—but the farmer strongly objected—Corrigan agrees to leave the lock off if he'll tell who turns off the water—The guy says it's the water dept. The water dept. says the owner, a "Switzer" in Paris, orders them to—upon contacting the town major we find out he sends a check once a month to pay the water dept. In other words, the owner is getting a "rake off"—

Added to this—it is increasingly difficult to make purchases in town— They close their doors on you—this is nothing compared to the madhouse in LeHavre—One incident: a bunch of G.I.s tried to take over a woman's house—a Frenchman coming to the rescue was fatally shot in the head and chest—another: a guard detachment gave their rifles to the German p.w.s— released them. The latter soon had a gun fight with the gendarmes!

Only solution—get us out of this—pretty soon they'll start another war and we'll never get home—much of this isn't in newspapers—but there is so much going on—it seems hard to believe it can be suppressed long—By the way—our gasoline was stolen a while back—so now they put on a guard—I go on every other night—I stay inside about 50 yards from the gas—good thing the gendarmes are around—

Told mom the one and only McKendry is back again—he has 60 points—hope I go home with 'im—"Edward Everett Horton" is on the radio—Overcast day—

Slong

November 9

Posa,

Hyars the song "Symphonie." French singer who sing this with Fernand Clare's orchestra is trying other US numbers—Helen Forrest style—is giving with right oomph at right time—but is giving with wrong syllawble—

Symphonie, symphonie d'un jour. Qui chante toujours
                              Dans Mon coeur
lourd. Symphonie D'un soir de printemps,
C'est toi que J'entends   Depuis longtemps

                                    Tes accords ont garde
leur parfum   Je revois des souvenirs defunts . . .

symphonie, symphonie.

Je revois les rideaux fanes—que pour nous aimer tu as fer mes. . . .
Dans la nuit tout commeau tre fois
Il trame par fois un peu de toi . . . Et les mots, et li son
de ta voix . . . maintenant Je les re trouveen moi
C'est fini, C'est fini
                    Et J'entends
grand a' l'fini—comme hue harmonie—Ma symphonie
              Ma symphonie . . .

LITERAL TRANSLATION

Symphonie of a day that is always singing in my sad heart—Symphonie of a day in Spring. It's always you whom I listen to. A long time your harmonies have kept their perfume. I see again old memories which are dead.

I see again the curtains which you have closed upon my love. In the night as in the day is something of you, the words and color of your voice. Now I find you again, but it is finished. Then once again the harmonie that is my Symphonie

November 11, 1945

To Mrs. Fanset
Watertown, South Dakota

Today, Armistice day, is filled with the memory of Jack—although it has been nearly ten months since I was last with him, I can still see his dark, impish eyes, his sincere, modest expression, his familiar swinging stride, and hear his inimitable rippling laughter—I was with Jack during his growing years, watching him drop his early shyness to emerge with an aggressive, sparkling personality. Mature and clear-headed, serious and gay—relied on and respected by his companions—We went a long way together from Fort Snelling to Germany. I remember Jack as the cheerful, dependable rookie, weathering the KP assignments with a grin, intently thinking ahead to the week-end.

Jack, Sid Ellicott and I stuck together and our bond endured throughout the months of training and combat—We spent many joyful days in Columbus, Georgia, Grenada, Mississippi and Memphis, Tennessee—Sometimes we even planned for and discussed the period following the end of the war—

Jack and I spent our twelve hours in New York together—In a vacant cabin on the Queen Elizabeth we watched the skyline of New York darken and fade in the evening and felt empty and uncertain—Next morning the US slipped behind and we headed out to sea—

Jack had strong hands and shoulders, an endurance and spark of vitality—that could send him thru the grueling hikes upright, seemingly unperturbed. He had a desire for knowledge that needed to be satisfied and yet he loved the land and freedom of the Dakotas and he relished the comforting thought of settling down. We sunned ourselves on the hatch on the top deck of the Elizabeth, airing our minds, letting our bodies exalt in the sea air and the overpowering magnitude of the ocean—Later on I remember Jack just as contented squatting in the mud in a sea of Machine Gun parts—confident that he could locate the trouble and make his weapon function smoothly—During the months of conditioning in England and Northern France Jack had become part of a team operating a 30 cal Machine Gun. During the listless, nasty months of St. Nazaire & Lorient Jack kept up his spirits and his singing helped to sweep away the gloom of his platoon. Occasionally we met and recalled the pleasant days of months before. In Perl, Germany, Jack joined his section members by wearing a purple silk scarf—Snow was on the ground, the sky and Jack were very bright as he showed me a recent color picture of his girl. Next morning our Company pushed off on our first attack—In the silvery hush of approaching dawn, we moved like ghostly forms toward our objective, Butzdorf. Jack had two boxes of MG ammo—He was walking beside me, his usual chipper self. I noticed how clean and well-groomed he was, even then. He reminded me of a story I used to tell at Fort Benning [The Two Blue Gnus and a Yak]. It was a satisfying moment of re-born friendship. On the fringe of a woods we paused to wait the order to advance. Soon the sky was ablaze with fire and smoke. There was no time for goodbye. Jack was needed. He bobbed away thru the trees and snow and was gone.

Two months later in England, Sid and I chanced to meet in a convalescent hospital—His shock was only dulled by the realization of what a mother must feel—But Jack's mother can certainly be grateful for Jack's fine sense of perception and balance—He believed in God and was faithful—But more than that he gave of himself—His generous optimistic nature earned him the everlasting devotion of his comrades—If greatness is measured in deeds and their value who then can say that Jack was not great?

NOVEMBER 11

Armistice Day—They ought to change it—First place—us soldiers—restless irritable, impatient to go home

Ho hum and all that—

November 13

Horstt—

—Still pulling guard at the motor pool—the dogs "Ox" and "Pisser" are so hungry they eat light bulbs and kindling wood—"Just their teeth coming in," I is told—weeded out two sachels of junk which is accumulating the last 15 months—mostly your letters—but some had to go—no more room for clothes in my duffle bag!

Nordic—Wrote Mrs Fanset on Armistice day—Year ago I rejoined my company near Lorient—Slept in a dug-out that nite—muddy water drippin' in. I'll never forget the reception I got—as I stepped out of the jeep—Jim McLees and a squad are pulling out—turn back to greet me—Fanset too—

November 16, 1945

BARENTIN, FRANCE

Sgniteerg!

Yesterday Captain Chaffin is coming up to pay us. Of the five some mille I collect (including 1500 in debts outstanding), I send home $80. Do to same as usual. This 810 I speak about is <u>no</u> <u>more</u>. It is entirely deactivated. As far as I know, I am now in Company "C" 3184 Signal Service Battalion, but <u>do</u> <u>not</u> use he as address until I let you know for sure. Chaffin is saying, furthermore, that 60 pointers will shortly travel up to <u>Bruxelles</u> (Brussels), Belgium. This does not make me too happy—I know when I am well off. I will <u>not</u> be home soon. The 3184 is another one of these "essential" outfits, with a tentative sailing date of March 2. The 60 points are supposed to leave before that, if that is any consolation.

At the moment I still pull my guard and wait for developments. The weather has provoked the AFN announcers to say "This is AFN, serving sunny Normandy" at station breaks. Guy wants to use this typewriter. More later.

'sall,

Mort

,

November 19

LILLEBONNE

Garlm [brother]:

I picked out a selection for you—including works by Voltaire & Balzac, a French love story, a murder story—an illustrated book on French artisans— Tres bien? Dont be too ashamed of your brother—but you probably know I know next to nothing of the French language—I know customs, manners, little peculiarities—differences of speech in various localities—a thousand more words and phrases than before I came over here—but I <u>cant</u> write or understand or speak the way a normal person should who associates with a people for more than a year (Picked up quite a bit of German from the PWS)—for the simple fact is I dont associate with the people—this comes usually in cafes—I dont get near the people except in business transactions, dances and such—Most of the French I know came from G.I.s who <u>do</u> get around (like McKendry) and from the little army booklets—McKendry got a pkge—"How dare they?" he shouts —He returns the pkge enclosing a note: "Keep out of my life forever!"

November 21, 1945

CAMP LUCKY STRIKE

Allo—

Arrived here this noon after two restful days at Lillebonne—At latter place we enjoyed the run of the Chateau: (810 has shipped out)—a shower—etc—our last luxuries .. shaved in green and white tile bathroom—slept in library—no mail— .. Can't understand how the army ever managed to find such places as this—We wind over the countryside—finally see a desolated looking mess of tents—At S-3 I sweat because we have no transfer orders—but they know we are coming—assign us to Co "I" 354th Infantry—Got settled at last—but the five of us were split up as the tents were filled—We have wooden floors and lights—also a stove—pws do most of the work—But we'll be pulling guard as per usual—Had cold spam, cold tomatoes . . .

November 22, 1945

CAMP LUCKY STRIKE

Bertsk:

Thanksgiving dinner was not half as nice as the one I ate a year ago in the rain and mud—But then I was on k.p. in the rest area—Living in a pup tent. The rumor says we're supposed to take off sometime between Dec 1 & 5—Much to be done yet—turning in—receiving clothing—SHOTS—etc Big—loverly JAP in my tent—last Thanksgiving he couldnt eat—cause he'd been shot in the mouth —"S&S" announces Robt Benchley's death—Just read "Benchley Beside Himself"—picked up new books—nothing much else to do—PASS, DAYS!!

November 24

CAMP LUCKY STRIKE

Luba:

Our processing is almost at an end—Had an influenza shot yest—Put shipping numbers on our duffle bags—Turned in currency exchange and pay books—Rumors as usual—are driving us cwazy—also millions of lil dogs— which bark 20 hours a day

goombye Mort

November 26

Werske—

In final processing stages—Met a guy from the 94th who had four pistols—
I got a bootiful Czechoslovakian 38 from him—Everyone is allowed to carry
home one weapon—I'm also bringing a set of draftman's tools—

November 28

STATEMENT OF STATUS

Lla:

Today is designated as our "readiness" date—we're ready, all right—As far
as I can see we're completely processed (except for more shots) Now there
is nothing to do except get lost in the old army game of hurry up and wait—
Lines stretch into infinity—the Red Cross is bulging—We keep happy
with talk—chess—books—and for some strange reason I got in the
communications platoon, which has a radio! It's a lovely day—think I'll
go surf board racing—

November 29

Allo

Gonna be an awful letdown if we dont parte soon—They've even told us what
uniform to wear on the boat! If they give us u.s. dollars—big pile o' gamblin'
will commence—27 days to Christmas—aint so important to me—but these
guys really have their coeurs set on that date!

It was once again across the channel, this time on the *Twickenham,* a converted
railroad ferry, to Southampton where I was to depart, finally, on the aircraft
carrier *Enterprise.* The channel crossing was "smooth," but my change back to
civilian life was a tremendous shake-up through fierce north Atlantic storms.

December 10

SOUTHAMPTON

Assorted:

. . . We decide to tour Southampton. The sun was out, I had my camera, but
there wasnt much to photograph—saw a beautiful school and arts building

where many children had perished in a bomb attack — The churches, of course, were other bomb devastation — Mc and Copp are looking for scotch — in one pub — an old woman tells us she had too much ale and guiness "down her neck." — "It's what you live for" — she says — We wind up near the Polygon Hotel — sit in the station — have tea and cakes — take off — get in London at 1820 — in the dark — I head directly for my old hangout "The Interstate" — a bit too late for everything — shows are filled up — the two boys get happy on 5 shots of scotch — I drag them around Leicester Square — Trafalgar — dead — so we go in The Rainbow — hang around listening to classical music — we are disgusted no little — as far as I'm concerned if I cant see a stage production in a "big city" snosense going — I dragged 'em out this morning — we tried to locate our captain to get an extention — no go — arrived at Waterloo in time to catch the train — but the idiots kept sending us back and forth from gates 9 & 10 — and the train rolled out — we took the next — Our transp cost us nothing — used a travel warrent — "Who's the ranking man?" the guy asked — "I am," sneers McKendry. "Private!"

December 12

Scone —

I must have a rugged stomach — had about sixty cases of ptomaine pizining after a dinner meal of meatballs — Mess is still best since Shanks (N.Y.) We've had our final customs inspections — and expect a physical (short arm) shortly — Still appears to be the USS Carrier "Enterprise"

Dec. 14, 1945

Southampton

ZZLT —

In about two hours I'm scheduled to take my feet off European soil — A little over six months ago I sat on my bed at the 826th Conv. Centr. and summed up before starting off on a new series of events — Maybe it's proper that I do the same now —:

The last six months have been about as mediocre as the time I described formerly. — All the beneficial traveling and sightseeing has taken place during this period, however. In spite of the small amount of education and experience I've been able to salvage on the continent, the desire for a quick transition from this world to the one I knew 27 months ago has only increased, and even now, as the climax approaches, it is difficult to express even an inkling of impending freedom . .

But I can never feel as low as I did last June 6 when I embarked for France for the 2nd time — We were herded around to a battered railroad station and took "forty and eights" to Etemps, France to report to the 14th Repo Depo — There, the weather was nice, and we were able to enjoy a short rest — I soon learned I was classified as 055 (general clerk) and it wasn't long before the duffle bag and pack had us sweating again — They sent us to a transit camp at Chartres, France, June 13, where we were assigned to barracks with wooden beds, wooden mattresses — We were glad to leave, and were even more pleased to find passenger accomodations for a journey west to Rennes (June 19) and the 3159 s.s. Bn. This outfit only served us a horrifying fact: it was Pacific bound.

We claimed ignorance of all parts of the Signal Corps, and after ten days, including a Sunday visit to Mont St. Michel (June 24) we were trucked up to the 810 s.s. at Cherbourg (June 29) — Latter outfit was scheduled to go home. A pleasant set-up was interrupted again. Down we went to tents and Isigny (July 3), on detached service to a p.w. administrative co., the 1682 L.s. We suffered here awhile, and as good things were next on our list, departed for Barentin (July 14) and Chateau Kohler, where I spent my most pleasant months in the army.

The time slipped by — I "chased" p.w.s — went down to Paris on a three day pass (Sept 27–30) . . . Two weeks later (Oct. 16) I made a two day motor trip to Liege, Belgium, and on Oct. 25 left for a glorious furlough to the Riviera.

By this time the extra five points I had acquired in the form of an oak leaf cluster was bringing results. I left the 1682 Nov. 19 via Lillebonne to the 89th Inf. Division at Camp Lucky Strike — We sweated out mud and discomfort until Dec. 6 — then crossed the channel once more on the "Twinkinham" Ferry to Southampton — The aircraft carrier "Enterprise" beckoned encouragement (Dec. 14) - - - ?

**Discharged
Camp McCoy, Wisconsin
December 30, 1945**

MORTON D. ELEVITCH

To you who answered the call of your country and served in its Armed Forces to bring about the total defeat of the enemy, I extend the heartfelt thanks of a grateful Nation. As one of the Nation's finest, you undertook the most severe task one can be called upon to perform. Because you demonstrated the fortitude, resourcefulness and calm judgment necessary to carry out that task, we now look to you for leadership and example in further exalting our country in peace.

Harry Truman

THE WHITE HOUSE

Acknowledgments

Thank you, too, Harry Truman
and all my fellow trainees in Fort Benning and Camp McCain,
most commendable and endearing veterans, living and dead,
of the 94th Infantry Division.

Jean Van Doren is the genie who uncorked the letters and persuaded me to transcribe and edit them. (Mistakes and inconsistencies in the originals have been retained and are entirely my responsibility.) Nikolas Elevitch, my son, scanned the graphics with assured and nimble fingers. Bernard Elevitch, my brother, who had received so many of the letters, absorbed their rerun with restrained good humor. My parents, Evelyn and Herman, meticulously saved them. Marian Young, my agent, gave them their first professional credence. Karl Kageff, their editor at Southern Illinois University Press, made the right choices with caring persistence. Andrew Carroll tucked one, November 23, 1943, into his monumental *War Letters* book and energized me with inspiring calls. That same letter ("This week they are teaching us to kill") introduced the *American Experience* documentary on *War Letters,* coproduced by Robert Kenner and Melissa Adelson, gracious communicators. Support was generous from Gregory J. W. Urwin; Stephen Ambrose and Michael J. Edwards at the Eisenhower Center for the Humanities, New Orleans University; Joan E. Denman at the Institute on World War II and the Human Experience, Florida State University; the Minnesota Historical Society; Tim Johnson, Curator, M. D. Elevitch Literary Archive, Special Collections and Rare Books, University of Minnesota Libraries; Emily Catherman, Exhibit Curator at Historic Oakview County Park, Raleigh, North Carolina; Bill Henderson, small press publisher and lead pencilman; Vivian Abitabilo, who provided valuable technological assistance; Philip and

Roberta Herman (camaraderie and camera); Reg Thayer, who loaned his dog tags; Marybeth Darnobid and Pamela Jacobs of the Palisades, New York, Free Library staff; the Two Graces, librarians at the Piermont, New York, Public Library; Owen McKevitt; Gladys A. Spratt; Sara Pearson; Mary Tremblay; Louise Schraa and family; my daughter Ilena, who brought me sustenance with fanciful breads from fiery ovens; and daughter Kathrin, who answered my question "Why am I alive?" with lines—and lyrics—like these:

> Pure creative soul standing in a field alone
> Two hands on a gun, lightning strike, blood for blood
> bodies of boys strewn across his path
>
> leading him toward
> the hard disembodied weapon
> he'd learned to become
>
> "Pure luck" he says
> "It's pure luck I even lived at all."

M. D. Elevitch is the author of two novels (*Grips; or, Efforts to Revive the Host,* and *Americans at Home*) and a book of short fiction (*Green Eternal Go,* to be expanded as *Single for Tonight*). He edited and published *First Person,* a journal of travel, memoirs, and humor, in the 1960s and has contributed fiction and criticism to many literary reviews, anthologies, and newspapers. Mr. Elevitch has written on his World War II experience only once before: a brief paragraph in a short story published in 1989. He lives in Rockland County, New York.

Cartoon signature with shadow profile on prisoner's box.
Photo by Philip James Herman.